THE COM

MEZE TABLE

THE COMPLETE
MEZE TABLE

Rosamond Man

EBURY PRESS · LONDON

DEDICATION

To my father, for making Arabia his life; to my mother,
for her enjoyment of its foods; to both, for giving me
the opportunity to live in 'that fabled land'.

ACKNOWLEDGEMENTS

To acknowledge everyone who has had a helping hand in the preparation of this book would fill many pages, but to all of them I give grateful thanks. Especially to those who suggested recipes for which there was, alas, no room on the table, with assurances that I, at least, enjoyed them. To the cooks of my childhood must go an immense appreciation for giving me such insight into the exotic world of the Arab kitchen.

To all the embassies of the different countries, many thanks for their patient answers to often seemingly trivial queries, and I am particularly indebted to Mrs Halet Coruk, Miss Renan Taşçıoğlu, and Miss Defne Akyol of the Turkish Embassy for their help on many of the finer points of that country's cuisine, language and history.

To Miss Partington of the School of Oriental and African Studies much thanks for the wealth of information from that wonderful library, and to the Islamic Culture Board, gratitude for permission to quote from Professor Arberry's incredibly informative and erudite studies: also to Penguin for permission to quote from N J Dawood's enchanting translation of *Tales of 1001 Nights*.

To my two editors must go thanks which know no bounds: Veronica Sperling for having the foresight, enthusiasm and endless tenacity to make this book a reality; and particularly to Caroline Schuck, not only for her sympathetic editing but also her constancy, patience and, above all, extraordinary ability to restore calm spirits where there was often despair. Without them, there would be no book.

And finally, to my faithful and – thankfully – ever-curious-to-taste companion in the kitchen, Willbond, a very special thank you. Not only for a sound culinary judgement but for a cast iron constitution which rarely complained at an extraordinary assembly of dishes, often at the oddest of hours!

For anyone who wishes to delve further into the huge cuisine of this area, I can only direct them wholeheartedly to the book which first stirred many childhood eating memories, and sowed the seed for my own collection of recipes – Claudia Roden's wonderfully extensive *Book of Middle Eastern Food*.

Published by Ebury Press
Division of the
National Magazine Company Ltd
Colquhoun House
27–37 Broadwick Street
London W1V 1FR

First impression 1986
Text copyright © 1986 Rosamond Man
Illustrations copyright © 1986
The National Magazine Company Ltd

ISBN 085223 546 1 (hardback)
    085223 591 7 (paperback)

Edited by Veronica Sperling and Caroline Schuck
Designed by Bill Mason
Illustrations by Anne Ormerod

Computerset by MFK Typesetting Ltd, Hitchin, Herts
Printed in Great Britain at the University Press, Cambridge

CONTENTS

Introduction

◆

The Middle Eastern kitchen has a vast range, both culinary and geographic. You may meet your first taste of it in Greece and Turkey, then continue on a huge gastronomic tour right round the Mediterranean to Morocco at the western edge of North Africa. You will be treading an historic path, for throughout time the peoples of the area have swept down one upon another, bringing with them certain cultural influences, leaving some behind on retreat, and taking others home as part of the booty of war. Nowhere is this more apparent than in the realm of food. Ingredients, their preparation and their marriages may vary, to a greater or lesser degree, from country to country but nearly always will there be a 'feel' of another nation, a whisper of an ancient civilisation, testifying to this constant ebb and flow of ideas.

The ancient Persians spread their influence first, c 500–400 BC, but then Alexander the Great engulfed the whole region, founding Alexandria on the way, then pushing the boundaries of his empire right across to India. Remarkable man that he was, on his death in 323 BC there lacked a strong successor and the empire fell to pieces while the boots of Rome started to march. The Hellenic civilisation however, lingered on for centuries, its gradual retreat bringing with it much culinary thought from India, most of which seems to have been deposited in Persia, where the Indian influence is still strong in the kitchen of today.

Meanwhile, Rome captured, fought and lost the Middle East – perhaps because she took more than she ever gave, and Persia rose again in the third century AD. For the next 400 years it was the era of the brilliant Sassanid kings and they spread their tentacles through Syria and Palestine to Egypt. Then the surge of Islam came, sweeping from Damascus in a mighty curve across North Africa to Spain and Sicily. Attacking too in the opposite direction, they conquered Persia and founded Baghdad as their capital in that vanquished land (now, it is capital of Iraq). Here grew the dazzling court – absorbing all that was great and glorious from the Persian heyday – of the Caliphs of Baghdad. For a while they reigned supreme and this was the era of The Thousand and One Nights, of great banquets and of court festivities which gave birth to the fabulous myths and folklore of ancient Arabia. Then the Mongols flew in (and out) and by the fifteenth century the Ottomans were on the move. Constantinople conquered, their empire flooded in all directions – up to the Balkans (where many dishes today still bear Turkish names), down to the Fertile Crescent, from whence they were only dislodged by the Arab uprising of 1916–17. They had time to weld their extravagantly luxuriant touches into the cuisine, then it just remained for the French to add a dash of sophistication, the Greeks and the Italians a cosmopolitan streak. Throughout the many tidal waves of history, the Arab identity has stayed firm, but taking from the invaders those aspects and ideas which have suited their personality – and their kitchen.

Meze is perhaps the most famous feature of the Middle Eastern kitchen, and its name is apparently gleaned from the Genoese spice traders by their Arab contemporaries. *Mezzano*, the Italian word for middle, was quickly swallowed into the many languages of the area, to re-emerge in a variety of confusing forms. *Mezedes* or *mezethakia* in Greece, *mezeler* in Turkey (usually abbreviated to *meze*), *al mezah* or *al maza* or *mezze* in the Arabic-speaking countries.

Whatever the spelling of *meze*, what is not in dispute is its essence and its versatility. Delicious *mezes* make their appearance at every café, in every house, on many a street corner. They can be anything from a small nibble of toasted pumpkin, marrow or melon seeds to a whole array of salads, pulse dishes, eggs in a multitude of forms, dips with a myriad spices, vegetables – stuffed and unstuffed, tiny *kebabs*, mounds of olives – from minute and gleaming black to enormous and pale green, speckled with crushed coriander seeds and finely chopped garlic: a mass of colour, tastes and textures but all chosen to complement and offset each other. Even apparent main courses can be served as a *meze* provided they are a replica in miniature.

Eating, and the sharing of food, with guests and strangers is a matter of honour – and a ritual – in the Middle East, and the *meze* table may often provide a stranger with his first taste of this enormous cuisine. For even a simple drink of iced water (simple to us, very precious to the Arab) or a cup of coffee, small and dark, will never be offered without an accompanying titbit of some sort, while many a formal dinner may well begin with a crowded *meze* table – from the simplicity of fine matchstick strips of cucumber luxuriantly floating in iced water to enormous stuffed aubergines, gleaming in olive oil. Not a few innocent travellers have been caught unawares, when, deliciously replete on a multitude of *meze*, they are graciously moved to another room for the dinner 'proper' to begin.

Even in the East however, *meze* are often served as buffet party food and for this they are ideal. Since invited guests may often bring another (uninvited) guest with them – indeed in Iraq it is almost assumed this will be so, such a guest affectionately called your 'slipper' (*qabqah*) and receiving no less warm a welcome than you – the *meze* table is a sensible way of coping with what could otherwise be a hostess's nightmare. The variety of dishes at such a feast will always be enormous, their ingredients and spicings differing slightly from country to country, and family to family, but few of these spices are unknown to us in the West. It is their usage, rather than their existence, that gives this gorgeous food its particularly Middle Eastern flavour.

And it is this food that I remember so vividly from my childhood, wonderful breakfasts of newly baked pittas stuffed with tiny black olives, misshapen tomatoes, sweet onions and heavy green olive oil. Lunches of long, thin *kibbeh* – minced lamb pounded and seasoned with pungent spices; mounds of fresh herbs mixed into chilled yogurt (hardly ever eaten for breakfast in the Middle East, although its cheeses are). Exciting excursions into the mysterious *attarine* (spice street) of the *souk* (market) with perhaps, the thrill of being allowed to buy a little twist of *dukkah* (mixed spices) to nibble on the way home. I spent much time in the kitchens of our homes in various countries and, watching the cooks lavish such attention and care on their food, one could not help but be imbued with a feeling of a very ancient, and much treasured, tradition.

Combined with the open and almost overwhelmingly generous hospitality that is so much a part of the Middle East, I can think of no more perfect introduction to that exotic, now sadly troubled, but extraordinarily magical part of the world.

> When to banquet we are eager
> Well the table floweth o'er,
> And the ready cook doth fill it
> With the choicest foods in store:
> Forth it comes with goodly burden,
> Garnished by his precious lore.[1]

Quantities and cooking times

The one aspect common to all Middle Eastern recipes is their vagueness. It is over this that I have spent more hours and careful calculations, to try and arrive at a reasonable Western equivalent, than anything else. '2 round cigarette tins, 4 hazelnut knobs, a handful (small), and 1–2 pinches, mixed with . . . the size of a hen egg, cooked on a good fire while rolling the pastry, and it will be ready. Will feed a family.' And yet, it is not so very illogical. The round cigarette tins in question held 50 cigarettes (the flat ones, 25) and after much juggling with cigarettes and containers I finally discovered it to be roughly 225 ml (17 tbsp): much easier to use the tin, especially when they were always available. As a child I was often asked to lend my hand and pick up as much as I could of the parsley or coriander, so that wasn't too difficult – my neighbour's daughter has little hands, and they are willing; they are equal to 60–75 ml (4–5 tbsp). The rest was subject to much experimentation, while the average Arab family not only included several children, but aunts, uncles, mothers and sisters-in-law, cousins, distant visiting relatives and also untold friends who might have been invited by any of the family, but who also might just turn up. The door is never closed. And an Arab would never dream of greeting an unheralded visitor with the words 'we were just sitting down to dinner' without an invitation to join them. So quantities are loose and infinitely expandable, and so is the cooking time. If the pot has to stay on the stove for five more minutes, because the conversation is animated, so be it. Apart from the little fried pastries, which must not overdo, most dishes will happily simmer for a moment or two longer, and if something must come off the stove this instant, it can be piled onto its serving dish and put on the table. Very rarely is food served boiling hot, and often the flavours are enhanced by a slight cooling. So, the Middle Eastern kitchen is very relaxed, if you haven't a particular ingredient, another can usually be substituted. A dish can often be gently poached on top of the cooker as easily as in the oven, or vice versa. And if you think a little more food is needed, there are always olives, pickles, cheeses waiting in their olive oil, extra *pittas*, another salad quickly made – a veritable storecupboard of standbys. It is a welcoming, and hospitable, kitchen and the *meze* table, in particular, is ever-flexible. The quantities I have given are for serving one *meze* as a starter, so a number may be expanded proportionately. Although, I warn you when a particular taste is found that suits one person's buds, even these quantities may be unreliable. I entertained a three-year-old recently who declared himself very content with the bowl of pumpkin seeds. It was meant for six.

DUKKAH
◆
Nibbles

Thereon impose a regimented line
Of almonds and of walnuts, flavoured fine;
With cheese and olives prick the points thereon,
And add the vowels of mint and tarragon.[1]

Everywhere you go in the Middle East, be it the bustling streets of Cairo or Istanbul, the old markets of Baghdad or Damascus, or for a leisurely stroll along the seafront in Alexandria, there will be scores of street vendors – tempting you with a myriad of tastes and smells. Among the most popular will be those stalls selling ready-to-eat snacks and nibbles – for the people of the Middle East have no inhibitions about munching on 'a little something' between meals. And when you see what is on offer, the temptations are irresistible.

Pyramids of olives, all shapes and sizes, in a rainbow of muted colours from palest green to shining violet and the blackest of blacks. Trays of seeds – from pumpkins, sunflowers and melons – dried in the sun, then roasted and spiced with garlic and salt. Mounds of gleaming golden beans – fried and dried – and salted chick peas. Small rounds of creamy yogurt cheese, floating in huge bowls of heavy green olive oil, waiting to be scooped out, drained and rolled in fresh herbs and spices.

Favourite of all, for me at any rate, were the little twisted paper cones filled with *dukkah* or *do'a*, wonderful mixtures of crushed roasted seeds, nuts and herbs. The aroma of garlic, coriander, sesame seed, fresh thyme, mint, wild marjoram, and sweet cinnamon filled the air and I used to take huge deep breaths, turning from one vendor to another until I felt quite dizzy, pleading that I would only feel better if I could have something to eat! There would follow a blissful 10 minutes of happy juggling with two or three tiny packets, firmly clutched in one hand, while the other held a still hot, newly baked *pitta* – to be dipped into the bowl of olive oil high up on the vendor's stand, and then into that little twist of paper, savouring each mix one by one, always leaving a morsel of my favourite until the last mouthful.

Nostalgia plays a great part in one's love of certain foods and almost more than anything else, these mixes take me back to my childhood days. I make them often and also serve them as a starter to a meal. Unusual and simple to prepare, they are a great inducer of conviviality as people try them, quickly finding the blends they like the best. They taste just as good eaten under the shade of the damson tree in an English country garden as they ever did in those hot Cairo streets.

♦

Humvs bil Bilh
Salted Chick Peas

There always seemed to be a huge pot of gently simmering chick peas on the stove in our Baghdad kitchen. Once cooked, they would be spread out on metal trays – burning hot from standing in the sun – and sprinkled with salt. By the next day they had shrunk considerably and were gloriously crunchy. A similar effect can be achieved in cooler climes by lightly frying the chick peas, then drying them out in a very low oven.

Some people like to scatter over a finely chopped garlic clove as well as salt before putting the peas in the oven. Dried haricot beans are often similarly served after a soaking, light boiling, then fast deep frying, and cumin seed can be used instead of garlic.

———————♦———————

SERVES 6–8
225 g (8 oz) chick peas, soaked overnight or
  2×400 g (14 oz) cans chick peas, drained
60–75 ml (4–5 tbsp) olive oil
Maldon or coarse sea salt
1–2 garlic cloves, finely chopped (optional)

———————♦———————

If using dried chick peas, first skim off any skins which have floated to the top of the bowl, then drain the peas and rinse in fresh cold water. Bring them to the boil in a large saucepan, well covered with water, and then simmer gently for about 1 hour until they are cooked. They may need a bit longer depending on age but you can easily tell when they are done as they will be soft to the bite. It's virtually impossible to overcook these peas in any case.

Drain them thoroughly and pat lightly dry. If using canned peas, rinse them in cold water, then dry. Heat 60 ml (4 tbsp) of the oil in a large frying pan, then add enough chick peas to completely cover the base of the pan and fry for 4–5 minutes, turning them around to brown them all over – chopsticks are the ideal tool for this.

Cook the remaining chick peas the same way, adding the extra oil if you need it, then spread them out on a baking tray and sprinkle generously with salt, and the garlic, if using. Dry them in the oven at 140°C–150°C (275°F–300°F) mark 1–2, for 15–20 minutes, until browned and slightly shrunken.

These salted chick peas are nice warm or cold. They get nuttier on cooling, you can store them for a few days in an airtight tin.

Falafel or Ta'amia
Broad Bean Patties

Almost the national dish of Egypt, where they are eaten for breakfast, lunch, supper and at any time of day. The Christian Copts claim the dish originated with them and during Lent, which they strictly observe, enormous quantities are cooked every day – not just for themselves but to be given to friends too.

———————♦———————

SERVES 6–8
450 g (1 lb) dried broad beans, soaked overnight
2 medium onions, skinned and finely chopped
3–4 large garlic cloves, skinned and crushed
small bunch of parsley, finely chopped
small handful of fresh dill, very finely chopped
Maldon or sea salt
15 ml (1 tbsp) coriander seeds, lightly crushed
cayenne pepper
cumin seeds
corn oil, for frying
To serve
lemon wedges

———————♦———————

Drain and rinse the beans, skinning them if very large. Either put them and the onions through a mincer – the fine blade, twice – or, much easier, put everything except the cumin seeds into a food processor and whizz until pounded to a thick pasty consistency. Form into small balls about the size of a walnut, flatten slightly, then dip each side into the cumin seeds, pressing the patties in between the palms of your hands to make sure the seeds stick. Leave, covered, for 30 minutes.

Heat the oil in a large pan until it's almost smoking, then lower in a few *falafel* at a time and cook for about 6–7 minutes until deeply golden. Drain well and serve with *Salata Tahina* (page 16), *Pitta* (page 98) and lemon wedges.

Dukkah/Zahtar Do'a
Spice Mixtures

This is the general name for the mixtures, endless in variety, of nuts, seeds, herbs and spices sold in little paper twists, to be nibbled at or eaten with *pitta* or sesame bread rings dipped into olive oil. The mixture is always a dry one with the nuts lightly crushed or very finely chopped rather than completely pulverised, so if using a blender or spice grinder just whizz it very briefly.

The secret is to release the flavour but not the oils, or the mix turns into a paste and will then go rancid if not eaten immediately.

Each family has their own recipe and favoured combinations, so experiment until you find the ones you like the best. Below are a few of my favourites.

Simsim wa Kuzbari
Sesame and Coriander Dukkah

SERVES 6–8
175 g (6 oz) sesame seeds
50 g (2 oz) coriander seeds
50 g (2 oz) hazelnuts
Maldon or coarse sea salt
coarsely ground black pepper

———◆———

Grill the sesame seeds under a medium heat for a few minutes, turning them constantly and watching they don't burn. Put to one side. Then grill the coriander seeds and hazelnuts, separately, again constantly turning them. Crush the coriander seeds first, either in a blender or spice grinder, then tip into a bowl. Briefly grind the hazelnuts, just to coarsely break them up, then add to the coriander. Lastly grind the sesame seeds, a few seconds is usually adequate or the oils will start to run. Mix everything together, and sprinkle generously with salt and freshly ground black pepper. You can, of course, make this in much larger quantities if you like, as it will keep almost indefinitely in screw-topped jars.

Lauz, Na'na wa Kuzbari
Hazelnut, Mint and Coriander Dukkah

Fresh mint gives the mixture a sweeter, more herby flavour, Eau-de-Cologne mint is particularly good.

———◆———

SERVES 6–8
225 g (8 oz) hazelnuts
50 g (2 oz) coriander seeds
45 ml (3 tbsp) dried or 90 ml (6 tbsp) fresh mint
Maldon or sea salt

———◆———

Grill the hazelnuts and coriander seeds separately, until browned but not burnt, then grind briefly. Mix with the mint and a good pinch of salt.

Kamun, Qirfa wa Humus
Cumin, Cinnamon and Chick Pea Dukkah

Either use Salted Chick Peas (page 10) – in which case leave them, covered with a cloth, for a few hours after drying out in the oven. Or you can buy precooked, salted and dried chick peas from many Greek or Cypriot delicatessens. They are much tinier than the home-made version, round, and white in colour.

———◆———

SERVES 4–6
60 ml (4 tbsp) cumin seeds
5 cm (2 inch) cinnamon stick
275 g (10 oz) Salted Chick Peas (page 10)

———◆———

Dry fry the cumin seeds, turning them around frequently until they begin to smell, then transfer to the spice grinder. Grill the cinnamon stick for a few minutes until slightly bronzed, then break into three or four pieces. Grind the cumin first, pour into a bowl, then grind the cinnamon until it's very finely broken up. Add to the bowl, then grind the chick peas and mix them into the bowl, stirring well.

Mannaeish Z-ahtar
Thyme and Pepper Dukkah

A combination much favoured in the Lebanon where wild thyme bushes cover the hillsides. I like to make this in small quantities so the full impact of the fresh herbs can be appreciated. Any leftover I pop into a jar and use for spicing other dishes. This *dukkah* is excellent with newly baked wholemeal bread and olive oil.

———◆———

SERVES 4–6
good handful of fresh thyme sprigs
2.5–5 ml (½–1 tsp) coarsely ground black pepper

———◆———

Chop the thyme sprigs into two or three pieces, discarding any thick woody bits of stem, then grind briefly. Mix with the pepper – start with a little at a time to see how much you like.

Simsim wa Taghar
Sesame and Hyssop Dukkah

A very old Palestinian combination, hyssop being a favourite herb. It has a sweetly-bitter flavour and is very easy to grow, given good drainage and a sunny position. But don't let it be too generous with its flowers or it will seed itself to death.

─── ◆ ───

SERVES 4–6
100 g (4 oz) sesame seeds
60 ml (4 tbsp) hyssop leaves, stripped from the stalks
Maldon or coarse sea salt
freshly ground black pepper

─── ◆ ───

Grill the sesame seeds, watching they don't burn then lightly crush or very briefly whizz in a grinder. Tip into a bowl, then quickly grind the hyssop leaves. Mix together with salt and lots of black pepper.

Ushb Taza
Persian Fresh Herb Dukkah

In Persia, fresh herbs are an essential component of almost every meal and large bowls of assorted herbs nearly always form part of the *meze* table. Many are endowed with magical qualities – particularly if women eat them with cheese and bread. This is believed to help them keep their husband's affections and deter him from looking for a new – and younger – wife.

I like to sprinkle this *dukkah* lightly with salt and freshly ground black pepper and have a pile of walnuts and sultanas in the middle, though this is not strictly traditional.

─── ◆ ───

SERVES 4–6
1 handful each of, or some of the following:
  fresh basil
  fresh coriander leaves
  fresh parsley
  fresh mint
  fresh dill
  fresh tarragon
  spring onions
  fresh chives

Wash and shake dry the herbs, trimming the roots off the spring onions and cutting off all but 5–7.5 cm (2–3 inches) of the green tops (keep these for another dish or for flavouring soups and stocks). Chop the herbs, not too finely, and arrange in a large shallow bowl, keeping the piles separate.

Labneh
Yogurt Cheese in Oil

Huge jars of small round cheeses, gleaming in olive oil and magnified through the glass of the jar, sit on every café counter and line the shelves in shop windows. Rolled in fresh herbs or paprika, they make a favourite Arab breakfast.

─── ◆ ───

Makes about 16–20 small cheeses
10 ml (2 tsp) salt
2.3 litres (4 pints) natural yogurt
fresh mint, finely chopped
fresh marjoram, finely chopped
fresh tarragon, finely chopped
paprika
olive oil

─── ◆ ───

Line a colander or two large sieves with scalded muslin or cheese cloth and stand over a large bowl (or two bowls). Whisk the salt into the yogurt, then pour into the colander. If you have a suitably placed hook, tie the four corners of the cloth together and suspend over the colander and bowl – this is not absolutely necessary but it helps the draining process. Otherwise, leave to drain overnight. By morning, you will have a soft creamy curd. Form into small rounds and place on a perforated dish or basket (I use small fruit baskets) and put in the refrigerator for at least a day.

The cheeses can be eaten now, sprinkled with herbs or paprika and a little more salt if wished. If you want to keep them, leave to dry out in the refrigerator for another 2–4 days, depending how creamy you want the end result to be. Then pack into a kilner jar, cover with oil and store in the larder. When you want them, simply lift out of the oil and sprinkle with the desired herbs. They will keep for several months – and they make lovely presents.

Buzur Qara Mishwi
Roasted Pumpkin Seeds

Very popular in the Lebanon, these nibbles can also be made using sunflower or melon seeds. If taking the seeds from home grown produce, wash them well and scrape off all the fibres, then dry thoroughly before cooking. I put them in the airing cupboard for 2–3 days but you could put them in the oven, at the lowest possible setting, overnight.

SERVES 6

225 g (8 oz) pumpkin, sunflower or melon seeds
2 large garlic cloves, skinned and finely chopped
Maldon or coarse sea salt

Heat the oven to 200°C (400°F) mark 6. Spread the seeds out on a baking tray, then dry roast them for 12–15 minutes until they are darker in colour but not too browned. Pour into a bowl, scatter over the garlic and a generous pinch of salt, mixing everything thoroughly. Cover and leave to cool. The longer you leave them the better as this allows the garlic to permeate the seeds. Overnight is ideal, but they can be eaten almost immediately if you wish.

Izgara Beyaz Peynir
Grilled Feta

A particularly delicious *meze* and much loved in Turkey where they used to serve it in small squares of very thinly battened silver. You can also wrap the cubes of cheese in tiny fresh vine leaves – fiddly, but worth the effort as the flavour is gorgeous.

In Egypt and Iraq, the cheese would be quickly fried in a little very hot oil, and in Baghdad sprinkled with lime juice. It is also delicious substituting a good matured Cheddar for the Feta, Hallumi or Kasseri.

Makes about 16–20 cubes

450 g (1 lb) Feta cheese, Greek Hallumi or Greek
  Kasseri
lemon juice
paprika (optional)

If the cheese is very moist, let it dry out for a few hours – but not more or it will crumble too easily. Cut into small cubes and either arrange on a grill grid or, better still, a barbecueing double grill as this makes the turning so much easier. Put under a hot grill for a few minutes until the cheese just starts to melt, turning over after 1–2 minutes. Serve immediately sprinkled with lemon juice, paprika if liked, and accompanied by hot pittas.

Coriander'li Zeytin
Coriander Spiced Cracked Olives

Huge pale green olives are marinated in oil with coriander, garlic and rigani to make this Cypriot favourite. They keep for up to a year and the oil is delicious for cooking.

Makes 2×450 g (1 lb) jars

450 g (1 lb) large green olives
45 ml (3 tbsp) coriander seeds
2–3 garlic cloves, skinned and finely chopped
30 ml (2 tbsp) rigani or dried oregano
about 300 ml (½ pint) olive oil

Cut a cross at the top and bottom of each olive, cutting right through to the stone. Grind the coriander seeds in a blender or spice grinder, then pack the olives into jars, sprinkling a little coriander seed, some garlic and rigani over each layer. Leave a good 2.5 cm (1 inch) at the top of the jar and then fill with olive oil. Cover tightly and leave to marinate for at least 2–3 weeks to let the flavours permeate.

T'atbil
Coriander and Chilli Mix

A spicing mixture, this time from Tunisia where chilli is often used.

SERVES 3–4

50 g (2 oz) coriander seeds
6 garlic cloves, skinned and finely chopped
25 g (1 oz) caraway seeds
1–2 dried red chillies, seeded and coarsely chopped
Maldon or sea salt (optional)

Dry fry the coriander seeds until the aroma develops, add the garlic and fry for another minute, constantly stirring so it doesn't burn. Tip into the spice grinder and blend briefly. Fry the caraway seeds and red chilli (use two, if you like things hot) then grind these briefly. Mix everything together and season lightly with salt, unless you are using the mix for spicing.

SALSA

♦

Dips and Sauces

On any *meze* table, there will be a multitude of small bowls full of soft, puréed mixtures – begging to be dipped into. Almost translucent aubergine, pale pink *taramasalata*, creamy ground almonds, flaming red chillies, stony-coloured tahina, the bright green of fresh herbs and glowing orange sauces – all will be artfully arranged on the table to best show off their colours and the textures of the foods they are to accompany. For many are not only eaten as dips, with bread, but are also there to complement meats, fish, salads and mounds of soft, fluffy rice.

Garlic, bread, potatoes, olive oil, eggs, lemon juice, tomatoes, and nuts of all sorts are transformed in a variety of ways to produce each country's specialities. Egg and lemon is a favourite in Greece, so too the thick, wonderfully garlicky *Skorthalia* (page 15). Garlic appears in many guises throughout the region – in a thin olive oil sauce and in a rich mayonnaise in Turkey; with tahina all over the Middle East; with hazelnuts in Iraq; with almonds in Syria, Egypt and Persia. Walnuts or delicate pine nuts dominate the sauces in Turkey while masses of fresh herbs are used in the Lebanon.

Yogurt knows no boundaries and a bowl of chilled, freshly made yogurt will appear on almost every table at almost every meal. Heavily laced with mint it makes a cooling salad. Cucumber is added in Turkey and Greece with lots of garlic, or sometimes a touch of tomato paste – to faintly tinge it pink. Paprika is also favoured in Turkey, usually mixed with olive oil and dribbled over in a decorative pattern – a much loved garnish for many dips, especially the earthy-tasting *Humus bi Tahina* (page 15).

Chillies make their appearance in Iraq, the Yemen and North Africa – it seems the hotter the climate, the hotter the sauce. The Yemen, with its sizzlingly high temperatures – you can literally fry an egg on a flat stone in the sun – has a sauce to match. An old recipe I have calls for two 'tinfuls' of dried red chillies – roughly 20 chillies – to two large tomatoes!

Perfection in the art of sauce-making must, though, go to Persia. Here fruits and meats are slowly simmered, enticingly seasoned with subtle spices – rose-water is often also added – and then served with their wonderful crusty rice, *Chelo* (page 94). Whatever else is on the Persian table, a dish of *chelo*, with a sauce, will invariably be there as well – a tribute to centuries' of experimenting in the kitchen.

Humus bi Tahina

Chick Pea Purée with Sesame Seed Paste

One of the most popular and well known Middle Eastern dishes – and rightly so, with its deliciously nutty, earthy flavour. Although there are canned varieties available now, which are perfectly passable, these pale into insignificance in comparison with the home-made version.

The garnish is an age-old one varied sometimes in Persia where pomegranate seeds are also occasionally used as well. In the Lebanon *sumac* is often preferred to paprika.

———————◆———————

SERVES 3-4

150 g (5 oz) dried chick peas, soaked overnight, or
400 g (14 oz) can chick peas
juice of 3 large lemons
125-150 ml (4-5 fl oz) tahina paste
3 large garlic cloves, skinned and crushed
Maldon or sea salt
pinch of cayenne pepper
To garnish
22 ml (1½ tbsp) olive oil
5 ml (1 tsp) paprika
30 ml (2 tbsp) finely chopped parsley

———————◆———————

If using dried chick peas, skim off any floating skins and debris, then rinse. Place in a large saucepan. Cover with water and boil for about 1 hour until they are quite soft. Drain and reserve a few chick peas for the garnish. Canned chick peas should be drained, then cooked in fresh water for 15 minutes.

Either put the peas through a mincer and then mash to a paste or put in a food processor with the lemon juice and 30-45 ml (2-3 tbsp) of the cooking water and whizz until puréed. Add the tahina (use the lesser amount with canned chick peas, adding more if necessary), garlic cloves, a large pinch of salt and a small one of cayenne and whizz again. Check to see if it needs some more salt, and maybe a little water if it is very thick, then turn the purée into a bowl. If you are making the dip by hand, add the ingredients to the minced and mashed chick peas, a little at a time, whisking well between each addition – the purée should be quite creamy by the time you have finished.

To garnish the dish: mix the olive oil with the paprika and drizzle it over the surface of the cream. Sprinkle the parsley on top and form the whole chick peas into a pattern on top – a star is often used.

Skorthalia

Garlic and Breadcrumb Sauce

The simplest version of this gloriously garlicky sauce is made with breadcrumbs, garlic, olive oil and lemon juice. It's a pungent and gutsy sauce – good with fried fish and strongly flavoured vegetables. For blander foods, I personally prefer the more refined version, given below, in which ground almonds are substituted for half the breadcrumbs. Both are ideal in very hot weather since they will not curdle or separate like mayonnaise, but I have another Greek recipe which does include egg yolks making it very similar to the French *aïoli*. Be warned though, it curdles extremely easily.

Should you wish to make the ultra-refined version using egg yolks, add them to the garlic, then beat the oil as if making mayonnaise before you mix in the breadcrumbs and almonds. Thin at the end with lemon juice or white wine vinegar.

———————◆———————

SERVES 4-6

3-4 slices white bread, crusts removed
4-6 large garlic cloves, skinned
salt
50 g (2 oz) ground almonds
about 150 ml (¼ pint) olive oil
juice of 1 large lemon

———————◆———————

Break up the bread, grind to crumbs in a grinder or food processor. Put into a bowl, cover with water and soak for a few minutes. Crush the garlic in a mortar with the salt until completely pulpy, then transfer to a large bowl.

Squeeze the breadcrumbs dry and mix with the garlic pulp, then mix in the almonds, stirring well. Add the olive oil, a drop at a time to begin with, then in a drizzle, and beat until the mixture is very thick. Gradually add the lemon juice, still beating hard, until the mixture resembles mayonnaise. Taste for sharpness, adding more lemon if necessary, or oil if you find it too sharp – the garlic has quite a tang. Serve with fish or vegetables. If you want to make it more of a pouring sauce, you can thin it down with cold water.

Tarator Sade

Garlic Sauce

This is a rich, and very garlicky, sauce from Turkey where it is used especially with fish and plain boiled potatoes. It is good with cold meat too.

SERVES 3–4

8 garlic cloves, skinned
Maldon or sea salt
45–60 ml (3–4 tbsp) olive oil
lemon juice
pinch of paprika

Crush the garlic in a pestle and mortar with about 2.5 ml (½ tsp) of salt, pounding it until it is really mushy. Very slowly add 15 ml (1 tbsp) of the olive oil, beating all the time, then gradually add up to another 45 ml (3 tbsp) of oil, constantly beating until it resembles a very thick mayonnaise. Season to taste with lemon juice – in Turkey they like it fairly sharp. I prefer a mellower flavour, so use your own judgement. Add more salt if need be, then beat in the paprika.

Salata Tahina

Tahina Cream Dip

The sesame seed paste called tahina must be one of the most loved – and versatile – ingredients of the Arab kitchen. Not only is it added to a multitude of other things, it is also, classically, served as a dip or accompaniment to most cold, and many hot, dishes. Although the basic ingredients for this are hardly varied throughout the Middle East, the proportions are very much a matter of personal taste.

SERVES 6

2–4 garlic cloves, skinned and coarsely chopped
Maldon or sea salt
juice of 2–3 large lemons
150 ml (¼ pint) tahina paste
1–5 ml (¼–1 tsp) cumin seeds
15–75 ml (1–5 tbsp) finely chopped parsley

Crush the garlic together with the salt in a mortar and pestle, then gradually beat in about half the lemon juice. Stir the tahina paste in the jar to mix in the oil which always rises to the top when the jar is standing, then measure out the desired quantity into a large bowl. Whisk in the garlic and lemon mixture, then add 45–60 ml (3–4 tbsp) of cold water and beat vigorously into the paste.

Grind the cumin seeds in a spice grinder, then add a little at a time, until you are satisfied with the taste. Add more lemon juice, and more water if necessary to achieve a thick-cream consistency. At this stage, it is very much what you like which determines how much you add. Sprinkle with the desired quantity of parsley and serve with Pitta (page 98).

Consbareyah

Pine Nut Sauce

In the Lebanon, Syria and Egypt this sauce is particularly popular with baked fish, usually served whole and often spectacularly decorated with huge radishes, olives, lemons or limes, fried pine nuts and tiny pickled cucumbers. Our cook in Damascus, passionate about his tiny patch of roof garden, also used to strew on rose petals.

SERVES 6–8

175 g (6 oz) pine nuts
2 slices of white bread, crusts removed
Maldon or sea salt
1 large garlic clove, skinned and crushed
juice of 1–2 lemons or 2–3 limes
60–90 ml (4–6 tbsp) fish, veal or chicken stock

Grind the pine nuts in a spice grinder until powdery. (Our cook used to very lightly fry the nuts in a little olive oil before pounding them. It gives a nuttier taste but it is not strictly traditional). Soak the bread in cold water for 5 minutes, then squeeze out the moisture.

Put in a blender with the nuts, salt, garlic and half the lemon juice and purée. Add a little stock (you can use water if stock is unavailable or you want to keep it vegetarian) and blend again. Check to see if you need more lemon or lime juice, adding if necessary, and then add just enough stock or water to make a paste about the consistency of barely beaten double cream. If you want to pour the sauce over say, a boned fish or chicken pieces, make it a little thinner. Otherwise serve in bowls.

Taramasalata
Smoked Cod's Roe Purée

Taramá is the dried, salt pressed and lightly smoked roe of the grey mullet. Since, even in its native habitat – Greece and Turkey – this has always been expensive, smoked cod's roe is often used instead. This produces the rosy pink cream so familiar now in the West, although some shop versions are such a pale pink they must be blushing with shame at their lack of the vital ingredient. If you should ever see a *taramasalata* glowing with a burnt-orangey colour, don't pass it by – for this will be made with the genuine mullet roe.

————— ◆ —————

SERVES 6
125 g (4 oz) smoked cod's roe
2 slices white bread, crusts removed
2 garlic cloves, skinned and crushed
½ small onion, skinned and grated
juice of 1–2 lemons
large pinch of paprika
90–120 ml (6–8 tbsp) olive oil
To garnish
black olives

————— ◆ —————

Skin the roe and either pound thoroughly to a paste or cut up coarsely and put in a food processor. Soak the bread in cold water for 5 minutes, then squeeze dry and crumble. Either beat into the paste or add to the processor.

If making by hand, add the garlic, grated onion and half the lemon juice and whisk it thoroughly, then stir in the paprika. Then add the olive oil, 15 ml (1 tbsp) at a time and alternating with 15 ml (1 tbsp) of cold water to every 30 ml (2 tbsp) of oil, whisking very well between each addition. Stop adding oil when the cream has the texture of a thick mayonnaise.

To make in the blender, simply add all the ingredients except the olives to the roe and bread, and whizz till you have a rich creamy texture. Add some cold water in proportion to the oil used and blend again.

Put the purée in a dish, smooth the top and garnish with the black olives. Eat with *Pitta* (page 98).

Nouggada
Almond Dip

A very delicate dip, also good served as a salad in the Syrian manner, with cold fish, poultry or their beloved *kibbeh*.

————— ◆ —————

SERVES 4–6
225 g (8 oz) ground almonds
2–3 garlic cloves, skinned and crushed
pinch of caster sugar
juice of 2 lemons
75–105 ml (5–7 tbsp) olive oil
Maldon or sea salt
freshly ground black or white pepper
60 ml (4 tbsp) finely chopped parsley
To garnish
paprika

————— ◆ —————

Mix the almonds with the garlic and a pinch of sugar. Stir in the lemon juice, then gradually whisk in the oil. Taste after 75 ml (5 tbsp) and add more if necessary. Season with salt and black or white pepper – or a bit of both, then sprinkle on the parsley. Dribble over a little more oil, then decorate with a pinch or two of paprika.

Teradot
Tahina with Walnut Sauce

Walnuts grow extensively in Turkey – where they are mixed with tahina to make a sauce traditionally served with cold baked fish. If serving with vegetables, some Turks use fresh mint to garnish the dish and add a little paprika.

————— ◆ —————

SERVES 3–4
175 g (6 oz) walnuts
juice of 2–3 lemons
75–90 ml (5–6 tbsp) tahina paste
3 garlic cloves, skinned and crushed
salt
45–60 ml (3–4 tbsp) finely chopped fresh dill or
  parsley

————— ◆ —————

Grind the walnuts in a spice grinder until they reach the gritty stage – take care not to over grind, you don't want a powder. Tip into a blender, add the juice of 2 lemons, 75 ml (5 tbsp) tahina, the garlic and a good pinch of salt and blend thoroughly. Season to taste with lemon juice and tahina. Tip into a bowl. Mix in the dill or parsley, leaving a little to scatter over the top.

Taratur
Walnut Sauce

Another sauce for fish from Turkey, this time without tahina.

◆

SERVES 4–6
175 g (6 oz) walnuts
juice of 1–2 lemons
45–60 ml (3–4 tbsp) olive oil
Maldon or sea salt
To garnish
finely chopped parsley

◆

Grind the walnuts in a spice grinder until fairly finely chopped but not powdery, then beat in about two-thirds of the lemon juice and 45 ml (3 tbsp) olive oil. Season lightly with salt, then check to see if more lemon or oil is needed, adding it accordingly. Thin with a little water to a thick pouring consistency, then pour over the fish and sprinkle with parsley.

Avgolemono
Egg and Lemon Sauce

The classsic Greek sauce for almost anything from fish to chicken and meatballs. The Turks are fond of it too – particularly for minced lamb meatballs. The one 'must' is that the stock should match the dish the sauce is being served with. The only exception is when serving with lamb meatballs – here water is usually substituted, as a lamb stock would be overpowering.

◆

SERVES 3–4
3 egg yolks
juice of 1–1½ lemons
150 ml (¼ pint) fish, chicken or vegetable stock
salt
freshly ground black pepper

◆

Beat the egg yolks until they are frothy, add the lemon juice – the greater amount for a really tangy flavour – and whisk again. Then slowly add the stock or you can use water, constantly beating. Season lightly with salt and pepper then either put over a saucepan of simmering water and stir until thickened, or put on a very gentle heat and stir until thick. Do not let the mixture boil or it will curdle, but if you are careful you can dispense with the double boiler. If in doubt, use it. Delicious with fish, meats, vegetables, stirred into soups or with rice.

Taratur Fendukh
Hazelnut Sauce

In Iraq hazelnuts are favoured for the sauces served with chicken and boiled lamb. I have also thinned this sauce considerably sometimes with chicken stock to make a delicious soup.

◆

SERVES 6–8
225 g (8 oz) hazelnuts
2 slices of white bread, crusts removed
2 large garlic cloves, skinned and crushed
juice of 1 lemon
Maldon or sea salt
about 120 ml (8 tbsp) chicken stock
15 ml (1 tbsp) paprika

◆

Grind the nuts quite finely. Soak the bread in cold water and then squeeze dry. Put the nuts, bread, garlic, lemon, salt and 90 ml (6 tbsp) of stock into the blender and blend into a thick purée. Add more stock until you have a thick but just pourable sauce, then mix in the paprika. If you want to serve this with hot chicken then warm the stock first.

Salsa Mishmish
Apricot Sauce

One of my most treasured memories of Damascus was walking through the orchards and picking up just-fallen apricots, still warm from the sun, soft, juicy and incredibly perfumed. (The unwritten law was that you never picked them off the tree – to this day, a law I find difficult to break.) Since apricots will not keep well, many found their way into the cooking pot, particularly for this sauce which greatly enhanced our rather stringy chickens. It is undoubtedly Persian in origin where it is usually served with lamb – indeed the two are cooked together.

◆

SERVES 6–8
45 ml (3 tbsp) olive oil
2 onions, skinned and finely chopped
225 g (8 oz) apricots, stoned or 125 g (4 oz) dried
  apricots, soaked overnight if necessary
3 cloves
5 cm (2 inch) piece cinnamon stick
2.5 cm (1 inch) piece root ginger, peeled and
  coarsely chopped
300 ml (½ pint) chicken stock
juice of 1 lemon

Heat the oil in a large pan, add the onions and fry gently for 10–15 minutes until golden and very soft. Add the apricots – with a few cracked stones if you wish – and turn them around until they are all gleaming and starting to go soft. Grind the cloves and the cinnamon in a spice grinder, then add the ginger and grind again. Add to the pan, then pour in the chicken stock. Simmer very gently, covered, for about 45 minutes until the mixture is very mushy. Add a little more stock or water if it becomes too dry. When very thick and soft, either pound with a wooden spoon until pulpy or quickly whizz in the blender – this makes a much creamier, smoother sauce. Add lemon juice to taste and serve with chicken or lamb.

Harissa
Hot Chilli Sauce

I have a Tunisian friend who can eat a whole bowl of this – admittedly a small bowl – neat! For less fiery mortals, the quantity below, which is about the least you can decently serve, will be quite adequate for people to dip into. Any left over can be stored in a small screw-topped jar. Cover the paste with a little more olive oil to preserve it.

————— ♦ —————

SERVES 4–6
24 red chillies, seeded if wished (I do, some don't)
2–3 garlic cloves, skinned and crushed
30–45 ml (2–3 tbsp) caraway seeds (optional)
Maldon or sea salt
olive oil

————— ♦ —————

Chop the chillies, then grind them in a spice grinder until powdery. Add the garlic and caraway seeds (plain *Harissa* is made without caraway but I think it vastly improves the flavour) and a goodly amount of salt – start with a generous 2.5 ml (½ tsp), and blend again. Taste by dipping in a piece of bread or raw vegetable to see if it needs more salt, then either tip into a small jar and just cover with olive oil until you want to use it: or, if using straight away, mix in a little oil to make a thick paste and serve in a small bowl.

Khoresh Portagal
Orange Sauce

This is my favourite of the famous Persian fruit and meat sauces which are traditionally served on their crusty-topped steamed rice, *Chelo* (page 94). Perfected and refined through hundreds of years, they are the pinnacle of the Persian kitchen with their subtle blends of delicate spices, fresh herbs, meats, fruit, vegetables and nuts. The secret of perfection lies in a very long, and gentle, simmering to achieve that delicate harmony and balance of flavours.

————— ♦ —————

SERVES 4–6
60 ml (4 tbsp) olive oil
900 g (2 lb) lean lamb, cubed, or chicken or duck
*   weighed off the bone, then cut into small pieces*
5 ml (1 tsp) paprika
5 ml (1 tsp) cinnamon
salt and freshly ground black pepper
freshly grated nutmeg
25 g (1 oz) unsalted butter
1 large onion, skinned and finely sliced
juice of 1 small lemon
5 oranges
75 g (3 oz) granulated sugar
75 ml (3 fl oz) cider vinegar

————— ♦ —————

Heat the oil in a large saucepan, add the meat and seal on all sides, then sprinkle on the paprika, cinnamon, salt and pepper (not too much pepper – the seasonings should be subtle not overpowering) and a good grating of nutmeg. Cover the meat with water, but only just, then simmer very gently with the pan covered, for 25–40 minutes until the meat is tender. Lamb will take longer than chicken or duck, and you may need to top the water up.

Meanwhile, melt the butter in another pan, add the onion and fry slowly until golden – but not quite brown – and soft. Stir in the lemon juice then reserve, off the heat. Once the onion is cooking, peel the oranges over a bowl to catch any juice drips. Take off all the pith and cut into segments, then make a tiny nick in each one to take out the pips.

Put the oranges in another small pan, sprinkle over the sugar, then pour on the vinegar. Let them stew gently for about 15 minutes, stirring occasionally.

Arrange the onion over the meat, pour on its pan juices, then pile the oranges on top and pour over the liquid remaining in their pan. Cover and simmer – extremely gently – for another 30–45 minutes, until the meat is meltingly tender. Serve with *Chelo* (page 94).

Mutabbul

Aubergine and Tahina Purée

A Turkish variation on a much-loved Middle Eastern dish said to have been invented by the ladies of the Sultan's harem – to win his favours.

◆

SERVES 6–8
2–3 large aubergines
3–4 garlic cloves, skinned and crushed
75–100 ml (3–4 fl oz) tahina paste
juice of 1 large lemon
large pinch of paprika
salt
To garnish
30 ml (2 tbsp) finely chopped mint or 15 ml
* (1 tbsp) dried mint*
olive oil

◆

Grill the aubergines – under a medium heat first, then a high heat after about 7 minutes, until well blackened and soft, about 20–25 minutes. Remove the skin while holding the aubergine under a cold tap, then gently squeeze to get rid of the juices.

Blend the flesh in a food processor, then add the garlic and 75 ml (3 fl oz) tahina and blend again. Add the lemon juice, paprika and salt to taste, then whizz until very smooth. Taste to see if you want to add some more tahina, otherwise pour into a bowl and sprinkle over the mint. Just before serving, pour about 5 ml (1 tsp) of oil over the surface. Serve with *Pitta* (page 98) or sesame bread.

Salkha

Herb Sauce

A wonderfully herby green vinaigrette from the Lebanon. Traditionally, the herbs were pounded in large pestles and mortars or between flat round stones but I make it in large quantities using a blender. It takes a matter of minutes and can be kept in a cool, dark place.

If you know you are going to want to keep the sauce, add slightly less oil than you will finally need and cover the dressing with a thin film of oil. I find if one makes this the day before using it, the flavours are considerably improved.

Makes a generous 600 ml (1 pint)
about 350 ml (12 fl oz) olive oil
Maldon or sea salt
5 ml (1 tsp) dry mustard powder
generous pinch of cayenne pepper
1.5 ml (¼ tsp) allspice berries
about 150 ml (¼ pint) red wine vinegar
15 ml (1 tbsp) chopped tarragon
15 ml (1 tbsp) chopped marjoram
15 ml (1 tbsp) snipped chives
15 ml (1 tbsp) snipped spring onion tops
15 ml (1 tbsp) chopped parsley
15 ml (1 tbsp) chopped chervil
5 ml (1 tsp) caster sugar

◆

Put the olive oil in the blender with a generous 5 ml (1 tsp) of salt and the mustard powder and whizz briefly. Add the cayenne pepper. Quickly grind the allspice berries in a spice grinder and add them to the blender. With the machine running, gradually add the vinegar, a little at first, then in a constant dribble. Put in the herbs and sugar and blend until emulsified. Taste to see if more oil, vinegar or salt is needed and adjust accordingly, then store in a screw-topped jar for up to one month.

Salsa Kamun wa Kuzbari Taza

Cumin and Fresh Coriander Sauce

We used to make this in Baghdad where coriander grew prolifically (it will flourish in England too, though vanishing for the winter since it is an annual: but it self seeds all over the place). It's a marriage between two powerful personalities so needs a strong-tasting partner: mutton or well-hung beef are ideal. So is raw cauliflower.

◆

Makes about 150 ml (¼ pint)
1 small bunch fresh coriander leaves
15–45 ml (1–3 tbsp) cumin seeds
Maldon or sea salt
good pinch of ground cinnamon
about 120 ml (8 tbsp) olive oil
30–45 ml (2–3 tbsp) red or white wine vinegar
pinch of granulated sugar

Chop the coriander leaves fairly finely, keeping the stalks for flavouring stocks. Grind the cumin in a spice grinder, then put in a blender with the coriander, about 1.5 ml (¼ tsp) salt, cinnamon and half the oil. Blend, and with the machine running, gradually add the remaining oil. Then, again gradually, add up to 30 ml (2 tbsp) vinegar, and a good pinch of sugar. Taste to see if you want more oil or vinegar, then pour into a bowl and leave for at least 2 hours to let the flavours amalgamate.

Laban

Yogurt

Yogurt and the making of yogurt, has been a part of everyday life in the Middle East for thousands of years. Originally, no doubt, a clever way of 'preserving' fresh milk (*halib*) which stays fresh with difficulty in those hot, humid climes, yogurt is now vital to the Middle Eastern kitchen. A bowl of chilled yogurt will always be on the table, spiced or plain, in cooling salads, lovely sharp cheeses, tenderising marinades, softening spicy stews, refreshing drinks. Yogurt is used every day and in every way. The perfect antidote to fiery temperatures, both meteorological and culinary. It is easy to make either in a thermos flask or, if you do not have one, a large bowl wrapped in a couple of towels will do, provided you give it a warm home for the 'making' period: an airing cupboard or the top of a solid fuel stove overnight are both ideal.

◆

Makes about 1 litre (1¾ pints)
1.1 litres (2 pints) milk
15–30 ml (1–2 tbsp) natural yogurt

◆

Bring the milk to the boil, then turn off the heat and leave it until you can hold your little finger, well dipped in, for a slow count to 15. If you want to use a thermometer, the temperature should be 41°–43°C (106°–109°F) so, by the time you have finished your count, your finger should be well pleased to come out. If the milk is too cool (or too hot), the yogurt will not thicken.

Beat your starter – this can be any plain commercial yogurt provided it has not been pasteurised, and spoon into a large thermos flask. If you use the lesser amount of starter the yogurt will not be quite so thick. It's still fine for salads, or marinades, or drinks but for making cheese (and my ritual breakfast bowl, with a little honey) I prefer the slightly thicker texture that 30 ml (2 tbsp) give. When the milk is ready, strain it into a jug and pour a little into the thermos. Whisk, using chopsticks again, then gradually pour in the rest of the milk, whisking all the time. You will almost feel it imperceptibly thickening while you stir. Screw on the top and leave for 8–12 hours. I usually put the flask by a night storage heater in the winter, but left it on the kitchen table once by mistake. The yogurt was still perfect. When you open the thermos, you will see a slight layer of watery liquid on the top. Unless you want to make cheese immediately, or need really thick yogurt, simply pour the whole lot into a large bowl and chill. Otherwise pour through a fine sieve, dropping the thick yogurt in the sieve into a second bowl every now and again as you pour. The thin yogurt can be drunk, after chilling, and the thick used as the starter for cheese. (It will of course need a further draining, see page 12.) The Arabs by the way do not discard the skin from the top of the milk. Mixed with a little sugar, it is considered a great delicacy, and in our household in Baghdad, the cook's mother – very ancient and disgustingly healthy – always used to be called out for her morning 'tipple', which she slurped down with great enthusiasm. Chilled, the yogurt will keep for about 1 week, although I confess it never stays around that long with me, and it is really at its best within 3–4 days. Just remember to keep back a couple of spoonfuls from the first batch to make the next.

SANBUSAK, BÖRĔGI WA DOLMADES

•

Stuffed Pastries and Leaves

> If thou wouldst know what food gives most delight,
> Best let me tell, for none hath subtler sight. ...
> Then, as thou wilt, in pastry wrap it round,
> And fasten well the edges, firm and sound.[1]

These are the glory of the *meze* table. In no other food is the Middle Eastern attitude of time, care, love and leisurely attention so visibly displayed. Tiny parcels, of soft dough, crisp golden pastry, brittle, paper-thin *fila*, darkly green vine leaves – all are filled with meat, chicken, cheese, eggs, fish, rice, onions, pine nuts, spinach, almonds, and sweet seasonings, to give a delectable mouthful – gone in an instant. *Börek, sanbusak, briouats, lahma bi ajeen, bstilla, briks, dolmades* – their names read like a Middle Eastern roll of honour. The shapes are varied, in size as well as outline – triangles, squares, coils, tiny flower pots, long slim fingers, envelopes, half-moons, truly enormous pies; each country, and family, clinging to their favoured design, and fillings. All have in common time and care lavished upon them; making the pastry, rolling it out – sometimes stretched onion-skin thin, cutting into tiny pieces, then grinding the spices, cooking the filling. Then lastly the stuffing, a hundred teaspoons or more neatly wrapped and arranged on trays, ready for the final frying or baking, an impressive centrepiece for the table.

The pastries are age-old, the poem describes in detail their making, which has hardly changed to this day. The leaves – vine, cabbage or spinach – and vegetables so loved for stuffing, courgettes, aubergines, tomatoes, onions, are a reminder of the Ottoman court. Endless banquets, and perhaps satiation, required a novelty, a tantalising enticement, a *bonne bouche* to whet the appetite. A wonderful combination of supremely sophisticated simplicity, all that is required of the cook is patience, and time. The results are elegantly satisfying, and always well received. No *meze* table should be without them.

Sanbusak – I

Cheese Pastries

At the end of our walk through the apricot orchards, if I had been very good, we would wander to the edge of the market where a street vendor sold these wonderful little half-moon shaped pastries – gleaming gold and warm from recent frying. They were filled either with a melting, salty cheese mixture or spicy minced meat stuffing sweetened with pine nuts, and I still go through the same agonies today in deciding which to eat first, which to keep for the last. For once one was bitten into, it was too more-ish not to go on.

The recipe for these has hardly changed from ages past, the dough in every country is rendered: '1 coffee cup of oil, 1 coffee cup of melted butter, 1 coffee cup of warm water, 1 teaspoon of salt. Add as much flour as it takes'.[2] The recipe my mother has from our cook in Damascus actually says '1 round tin full of oil, etc. etc.' referring to the cigarette tins he used as a measure – but then he did make enormous quantities of the things! Interestingly the method of decoration does not seem to have changed much either. I can remember thinking how ingenious 'my' street vendor was in marking his pattern on the half-moons with a nail. Then when I came upon Professor Arberry's treatise, I found the poem by Ibn Ibrahim, and in it quite clear instructions: 'Then with the rolling-pin let it [the dough] be spread and with the nails its edges docketed.' It is this sense of early sophistication, and the continuity with the past, that I find so fascinating about Arab cookery.

————————◆————————

Makes 15–18 pastries
For the pastry
50 g (2 oz) unsalted butter
50 ml (2 fl oz) olive oil
2.5 ml (½ tsp) Maldon or sea salt
about 225 g (8 oz) flour
30–45 ml (2–3 tbsp) sesame seeds
1 egg, beaten (optional)
olive oil, for deep frying (optional)
For the filling
225 g (8 oz) Feta or Hellim cheese
1 egg, separated
30 ml (2 tbsp) finely chopped fresh mint or 15 ml
(1 tbsp) dried
freshly ground white pepper

Put the butter into a small heavy pan and melt gently, taking care not to let it bubble, then mix in the oil and 50 ml (2 fl oz) of warm water and take off the heat. I'm afraid I may shock the traditionalists next because I use a food processor to mix the dough. It is much quicker, less messy and I, at any rate, get better results. For the dough has to be soft, but very well mixed yet handled as little as possible. So, if you do mix by hand, use a very large bowl and bear that in mind. Pour the warm butter and oil mixture into the food processor, add the salt and whizz for a second. Then pour a little flour in and whizz again. Gradually add up to 225 g (8 oz) of flour, whizzing constantly towards the end. The dough should be very soft – almost like a soft pastry, and leave the sides of the bowl clean. Take it out and put on a lightly floured surface. If it feels too greasy, lightly and gently work in a spoonful or so more flour. Break into four equal-sized pieces, then roll each one, on a floured surface, quite thin and cut out rounds – roughly 7.5 cm (3 inches) in diameter. Now, if you are going to fry the pastries, which I think is marginally more-melt-in-the-mouth, but undoubtedly more calorific and harder work, but it's the way I remember them, spread the sesame seeds over a large flat surface and dip the bottom of the rounds in the seeds, very lightly pressing them down so the seeds stick on. If you're going to bake them, hang on.

Make the filling by crumbling or grating the cheese – Feta may need to be mashed a little with a fork, then mix with the egg yolk, mint and a generous seasoning of white pepper. The mixture should be soft but not sloppy, if it is very thick though – and this will depend a bit on the cheese, mix in 5 ml (1 tsp) or so of the egg white until it is not quite at the 'dropping' stage. Put 5 ml (1 tsp) of filling on each pastry round, slightly off centre, and fold over the pastry to make a semi-circle – don't press the filling down too much, it shouldn't reach the sides or it can burst during the cooking. Seal the edges firmly and indent with a fork or nail, if you wish (I have a special 'baking' nail for this – it makes one feel somewhat historic, idiotic really). If baking, put the pastries on an ungreased and unfloured baking tray – they won't stick. Brush with the beaten egg, and then sprinkle with sesame seeds. Bake at 180°C (350°F) mark 4 for 30–40 minutes until they are delicately golden and lift up easily from the tray. For frying, heat a good 5 cm (2 inches) of oil in a deep pan. Cook the *sanbusaks* – a few at a time – in hot but not smoking oil for 3–5 minutes until golden brown and crispy. Drain well. Either way, enjoy them.

23

Sanbusak – II
Meat Filled Pastries

This meat filling is equally popular in Syria, Lebanon and Egypt. With pine nuts was the way my Damascus pastries were filled, but in Lebanon I also had a version which included poached brains mashed with the minced meat giving a softly creamy feel, slightly moister than the plain meat variety. There is also a recipe which calls only for brains, which I confess I've never had. However, since *briouats* with brains are delicious (page 27), I should think it is very good – you would probably need about 350 g (¾ lb) of brains, maybe a bit less. Wash them, taking off the outer membranes, then poach with a dash of vinegar for about 10 minutes, before mashing with chopped herbs, salt and pepper. If you want to use brains, omit the pine nuts in the filling.

————— ◆ —————

Makes 15–18 pastries
sanbusak pastry *(page 23)*
For the filling
15 ml (1 tbsp) olive oil
1 medium onion, skinned and very finely chopped
2.5 ml (½ tsp) ground cinnamon
1.5 ml (¼ tsp) ground ginger
freshly ground allspice
pinch of caster sugar
225 g (8 oz) lamb, minced
30 ml (2 tbsp) pine nuts
Maldon or sea salt
freshly ground white pepper
juice of ½ lemon

————— ◆ —————

Prepare the pastry and cut it out as in the previous recipe (page 23)

Make the filling: coat the bottom of a frying pan with the oil, add the onion and cook, very gently, for about 10 minutes until it's quite soft. Sprinkle over the cinnamon, ground ginger, a fair bit of freshly ground allspice and the sugar and stir for another 2 minutes. Then add the meat and cook until it's coloured, 4–5 minutes, then stir in the pine nuts and fry until they become pinky. Season with salt and freshly ground white pepper, then stir in the lemon juice and 30 ml (2 tbsp) of water to moisten. The mixture shouldn't be too wet, on the other hand if it's too dry, it'll just crumble. Simmer for another 3–4 minutes until the meat is juicy but not liquid. Cool for 10 minutes before stuffing the pastries. Cook as in the previous recipe, omitting the sesame seeds.

Lahma bi Ajeen
Arab Pizza

Not strictly speaking a pastry, this Arab pizza can be reheated at the last moment and is ideal for parties. Also called *lahmajoun* (pronounced the same in Turkish but spelt *lahmacun* – the 'c' without a cedilla sounded hard, as 'j'), this is the Arab answer to the pizza – in miniature, and cooked very quickly so that the base is still white and soft, perfect for folding over to eat easily, and instantly. They can also be warmed up in a moderate oven for a few minutes, which is ideal for parties. (I put them on a baking tray and cover them in foil, to keep them supple.)

————— ◆ —————

Makes about 20 pizzas
225 g (8 oz) plain flour
2.5 ml (½ tsp) Maldon or sea salt
5 ml (1 tsp) Easy Blend yeast (page 107)
15 ml (1 tbsp) olive oil, plus extra for greasing
For the filling
15 ml (1 tbsp) olive oil
1 large onion, skinned and chopped
450 g (1 lb) lean lamb or beef, minced
1 large beef steak tomato, blanched and skinned, or
  2 canned plum tomatoes
15 ml (1 tbsp) cumin seeds, ground
pinch of caster sugar
freshly ground allspice
Maldon or sea salt
freshly ground white or black pepper
30–45 ml (2–3 tbsp) finely chopped coriander
  leaves or parsley
15 ml (1 tbsp) tomato purée
juice of ½ lemon
25 g (1 oz) pine nuts (optional)

————— ◆ —————

Sift the flour into a large bowl or food processor. Sprinkle on the salt and the yeast and mix. Dribble the oil over the flour, then gradually add 150 ml (¼ pint) of warm water, constantly mixing or with the machine running, until a soft dough is formed. Knead hard for 10–15 minutes or whizz the machine for 3–4 minutes until the dough is very elastic and leaves the bowl clean. (Even though I do use a food processor for this, I still in fact then knead for 1–2 minutes by hand – lightly flour your hands first – it makes the dough very light and supple.) Brush a clean bowl with oil, then turn the ball of dough in it so it's thoroughly coated – this prevents the upper surface from drying out. Cover with a cloth and leave in a warm place for 1½–2 hours until the dough has doubled in size.

Heat the oil and cook the onion for 5–6 minutes until soft but not coloured. Drain thoroughly, then put in a large bowl. Add the meat. Chop the tomato, discarding the excess juice, then add with the cumin seeds, sugar, allspice, salt, pepper and coriander leaves. Mix the tomato purée with the lemon juice and stir in. I now also add pine nuts – traditionally either tomatoes or pine nuts are used but I happen to like both. Mix everything together very well. Don't worry if the mixture seems a bit dry – you do not want too much liquid or you'll have soggy pizzas.

Knock back the risen dough a few times, then divide the mixture into four pieces, and each of those into 5–6 lumps. Roll into a small ball, then flatten between your hands and gently pull out to make a circle roughly 10 cm (4 inches) in diameter. Or you can using a rolling pin – roll quite thin, but I quite enjoy doing this by hand. There is a mild challenge to see how thin, and evenly sized, one can make them! Arrange on a lightly oiled baking tray, then spread a little filling all over each circle. Go right to the edges, not only to keep the pizzas soft but to make them look enticing. Bake for 7–10 minutes in the oven at 210°C (425°F) mark 7 – the bases should be soft but cooked through. Serve hot or warm with lots of salad.

Heat 15 ml (1 tbsp) of oil in a pan, and sweat the onion in it for about 10 minutes until softened but not too coloured. Drain and mix into the fish, then add the parsley, half the lemon juice and season with salt, pepper and cayenne, if using. Taste and add more lemon if necessary.

Brush one sheet of the *fila* with a little oil, cut in half and place one half on top of the other. Spread some of the filling about 7.5 cm (3 inches) from one of the shorter ends of the *fila* strip. I make a slight hollow with the back of a spoon so the egg doesn't float about too much, then break the egg on top of the filling. Carefully, fold over the end of the *fila* to cover, then gently fold in the right and left edges to seal the sides, and quickly bring the long edge back (over the filling) and then roll completely up. Fill the remainder in the same way.

Fill a large deep pan with a good 5 cm (2 inches) of oil and heat gently. The oil should be hot but not smoking. Carefully lower 2–3 *briks* into the pan and cook gently until golden, turning over once, about 2–3 minutes each side should be sufficient to lightly set the eggs without burning the *fila*. Drain well on absorbent kitchen paper and serve hot.

Briks à l'Oeuf
Tunisian Stuffed Pastries

Be gentlemanly when you serve this Tunisian speciality – and warn your guests! For the innocent-looking *fila* envelope contains not only a delicious tuna and onion mixture – but a whole egg slipped on top just before the parcel is folded. The eating technique, sitting with your head thrown back, is soon acquired but I must admit the preparation terrified me for ages. Then I took the plunge, and it was really quite simple.

SERVES 6
peanut oil
1 large onion, skinned and finely chopped
175 g (6 oz) canned tuna fish, drained and mashed
small bunch parsley, finely chopped
juice of ½–1 lemon
Maldon or sea salt
freshly ground black pepper
pinch of cayenne pepper (optional)
6 sheets fila pastry
6 eggs

Börek

Turkish Stuffed Pasties

In Turkey, little stuffed pasties are called *börek*. They come in many shapes from fat squares or triangles for a family lunch to long slim fingers or 'cigarettes' for a more formal party. The fillings are varied, and so is the pastry. It can be a shortcrust, with or without eggs (I have even seen a plain flour and water dough in some recipes). More rarely it can be a pizza dough, similar to the one used for *Lahma bi Ajeen* (page 24). Lighter are those made with a flaky or puff pastry, while most delicious of all, to my mind, are those using the paper thin sheets of *fila* pastry (*phyllo* to the Greeks, *yufka* to the Turks, *brik* to the Tunisians and *ouarka* to the Moroccans). How a simple mixture of flour and water can be transformed merely by kneading, flattening and stretching – until you can almost see through it – is something that never ceases to amaze me. Thankfully, though, there are the experts, and *fila* is quite widely available, in packets of 12 or 24 sheets, usually 30.5×51 cm (12×20 inches) in size although this does vary considerably. Rolled and sealed in polythene they will keep in the refrigerator for 6–7 days (I have kept it longer but it was a bit brittle). But it freezes well, and almost for ever. Gentle, completely thorough defrosting is essential however otherwise it will just break when you use it. I tend to buy it in 450 g (1 lb) packets – 20–24 sheets – then divide that up into parcels of 5–6, immediately rerolling and sealing in polythene before freezing. Provided you always make sure it's quite pliable before starting, and keep sheets not actually being filled covered with a damp cloth, it is easiness itself to work with. The result is so light, without the extra richness of puff pastry, that I think it justifies the minimal effort involved. Having said all that, I do also use flaky or puff pastry sometimes, and very good it is too. Again, I tend to take a short-cut here, especially as I often make *böreks* in the summer, when the hot weather can cause havoc with pastry-making. But a good commercial brand, rolled out, then dotted with a little butter over two-thirds of the rectangle, folded into three and chilled before a final rolling out, produces excellent results. As a rule 450 g (1 lb) of pastry will make about 30–36 *böreks*, depending on size and shape.

Makes 18 **böreks**
450 g (1 lb) fresh spinach or 225 g (8 oz) frozen
25 g (1 oz) unsalted butter
100 g (4 oz) Feta cheese
30 ml (2 tbsp) walnuts, chopped finely
1 small egg, beaten
freshly ground allspice
freshly ground black pepper
225 g (8 oz) fila pastry
oil, for brushing and frying

If using fresh spinach, wash, trim and finely chop it otherwise defrost the frozen spinach, then stew gently with the butter and 30 ml (2 tbsp) of water until tender. Crumble the cheese and add to the pan with the walnuts. As the cheese starts to melt, stir in the beaten egg and cook for another 2–3 minutes. Season with allspice and black pepper, you won't need salt as the cheese provides enough, and leave to cool while you organise the pastry.

Have a damp, not soaking wet, clean cloth to hand. Take out one sheet of *fila*, roll up the rest, and cover lightly with the cloth. Cut the *fila* into long strips roughly 7.5 cm (3 inches) wide, and lightly brush each strip with a little oil. If your *fila* is the standard size of 30.5×51 cm (12×20 inches) you will need one strip per *börek*. If, however, you find – as I did recently – that it is approximately 35.5 cm (14 inches) square, then I think you need two. (Either way, the weight given should make 18–20 *böreks*.) So, if necessary, lie one strip on top of another. Then put a good 5 ml (1 tsp) of filling at one end, about 2.5 cm (1 inch) from the short side and slightly off centre (I work from left to right, so would place it nearer the top edge). Then lift the bottom corner up to meet the long top edge, making a triangle. You then lift the whole triangle to the right – you now have a straight edge on the left. Take the top left hand corner and fold this over to meet the long bottom edge. Again lift the complete triangle and fold over the right, and so on, until you come to the end of the strip. Either tuck in the leftover *fila*, or just fold over and press it lightly down, brushing with a tiny bit more oil, if necessary to make it stick. (This is much more complicated to describe than do – try it first with a long strip of paper!)

You can now either fry or bake the pastries, on a greased baking tray, at 190°C (375°F) mark 5 for about 20–30 minutes until they are lightly golden on top. Keep checking as ovens vary so much. I prefer to fry mine, unless I am making enormous quantities when obviously the oven is easier. Heat a good 2.5 cm (1 inch) of oil in a large deep pan until not quite smoking hot (a piece of broken *fila* will sizzle and colour in about 30 seconds), then add a few *börek* at a time, and fry, turning once, until golden all over. Lift out quickly – they brown in an instant, and drain well. You can, if you like, keep them warm in a very low oven while finishing the rest but I find that if you do about 4 at a time, the first are still warm by the end, so hot are they when they come out of the pan.

Sigara Böregi
'Cigarette' Böreks

These are *böreks* rolled up in the shape of a small cigar. Traditionally a cheese filling, similar to the one for *Sanbusek* (page 23) is used. You will need to cut the *fila* into rectangles 10 cm (4 inches) wide by 30.5–35.5 cm (12–14 inches) long, using 1 sheet per cigar. Spread 5 ml (1 tsp) of filling in a long thin line about 1 cm (½ inch) away from the shorter edge, roll over a couple of times, then fold over the long sides to enclose the stuffing, and continue rolling as if making a cigar. You will probably get more cigarettes than triangles out of the same *fila*, up to 24, so increase the quantities of filling slightly.

Burma Börek
Coiled Böreks

There is another shape often used for spinach fillings, which never fails to impress. But it absolutely has to be made with very pliable *fila* – I don't even use very slowly defrosted pastry as it can prove unreliable. So, when you have very fresh *fila*, make these lovely coils. Roll a long cigar, using half a large sheet of *fila* and having spread your filling – a good 15 ml (1 tbsp) or more – in a long, thin line down the longest side of the sheet, then very carefully coil the cigar round and round itself, making a spiral. These have to be baked otherwise they unroll, and should be packed tightly on the greased sheet. Once cooked, the danger is over. Start checking their colour after 15 minutes. Many people omit the cheese from this filling, substituting a finely chopped onion, and adding a few more nuts (pine nuts are nice) and some sultanas. In this case, don't forget also to add some salt. Again, 225 g (8 oz) of *fila* will make about 18 coils.

Briouats
Moroccan Fila Pastries

The slight variation in the name, once again, betrays the influence of the French in Morocco, but the little *fila* parcels are just as popular here as elsewhere in the Middle East. Squares, cigars and triangles are the shapes used – with a wonderful variety of fillings. The Morrocan imagination is given full rein here, for the stuffings are not only savoury but sweet too. A particularly glorious one is made from a ground almond and beaten egg paste, the *briouats* being dipped in boiling honey once fried, then left to cool. Even savouries are often given a sweet touch, parcels filled with a minced meat filling, or rice simmered in milk and butter with almonds, being lightly dusted – after cooking – with icing sugar and ground cinnamon. Surprisingly good. The most delicious *briouats* though, to my mind, are those filled with poached, fried brains (egged and floured first) and – best of all – those with *merguez*, the tiny but bitingly hot sausages. I have substituted *chorizo* (the hotter variety) quite successfully for these, cutting the sausage into four lengthways (to make a small 'cigarette') and sprinkling the pastry – before rolling – with finely chopped parsley – and sometimes a little cayenne pepper for extra spice. Wonderful.

Spanakopitta and Tyropitta
Greek Spinach and Cheese Pies

Spanakopitta is traditionally made with spinach and Feta cheese, while *Tyropitta* has a cheese and egg filling. For 12 sheets of *fila*, you'll need about 1.1 kg (2½ lb) spinach plus 175 g (6 oz) Feta cheese, while for the cheese stuffing 500 g (1¼ lb) Feta cheese, and 3 large eggs should be sufficient. Nutmeg and cinnamon are the preferred spices for the former, finely chopped fresh herbs for the latter. Bake at 190°C (375°F) mark 5 for 40–45 minutes and then at 220°C (450°F) mark 8 for 5–6 minutes to brown. Both these pies can, of course, be made in small triangular versions – *trigona spanakopittes*, and *trigona tyropittes* respectively in Greek. These should be baked at 190°C (375°F) mark 5 for 20–30 minutes.

Dolmas

Stuffed Vine Leaves (Hot)

Named after the Turkish verb 'to stuff', these enticing little rolls, smoky in flavour from the vine leaves, appear on tables throughout the Middle East. In winter, spinach and cabbage leaves are often used instead, while an elegant variation in Cyprus uses the beautifully marbled leaves of the tiny wild cyclamen. This is taboo in my house, since I spend my life encouraging the little creatures to increase – their minute flowers, purest white and brilliant pink, being one of the jewels of the winter garden. But it's a delightful notion – if fiddly, for I doubt that their largest leaves would hold even 5 ml (1 tsp) of stuffing. However, I am lucky enough to have access to a fresh vine, and all through the summer wonderful flat, fat packages arrive through the letter box – leaves, large and small, tenderly packed in tissue paper by my thoughtful cousin. A good wash, a quick blanching and they're ready for the freezer – carefully stored quite flat so they don't crumble once frozen; even more than with *fila* pastry is a gentle defrosting necessary since they are very brittle. Packets of leaves in brine are now widely available if you haven't a vine to raid and these keep well in the refrigerator, although once opened you should use them within a couple of days or they will dry out. *Dolmas* are served hot and cold, usually stuffed with meat for the former, rice in the latter. Both can be cooked, then frozen so it's worth making quite a large quantity at one time: open-freeze, then pack in dozens so you can take out a few at a time.

◆

Makes 30–36 dolmas

40–45 large vine leaves
125 g (4 oz) long grain rice
225 g (8 oz) lamb, minced
1 medium onion, skinned and grated or minced
1 large tomato, blanched, skinned and chopped
small bunch parsley, finely chopped
15 ml (1 tbsp) dried mint
5 ml (1 tsp) ground cinnamon
2–6 garlic cloves, skinned
Maldon or sea salt
freshly ground black pepper
juice of 1–2 lemons
30–45 ml (2–3 tbsp) tomato purée

Packeted vine leaves need soaking in boiling water for 30 minutes, then draining and soaking in fresh cold water for another 5 minutes. Fresh leaves should be blanched in a large pan of boiling water – 3–5 minutes will usually be sufficient to make them go limp, then drain and rinse in cold water.

Wash the rice by pouring boiling water over it, leave for 5 minutes, then rinse well in cold water and drain thoroughly. Mix in a large bowl with the lamb, onion, tomato, herbs and spices, then season with salt and pepper.

To stuff the leaves, lay them on a flat surface, veins facing upwards. Snip off the stalks then put about 5 ml (1 tsp) of the filling in the middle of the leaf, slightly nearer to the stalk end than the tip. Fold up the bottom edge of the leaf, then fold over the left and right sides to cover the filling, and continue rolling up to the tip. Put on a plate, tip underneath so it doesn't unroll again – it also helps to slightly squeeze each roll before stacking. Allow a few extra leaves in case of tears, but once you've done a few, you'll slip into the technique easily.

Line a large heavy saucepan with a layer of leaves, then arrange the rolls tightly side by side – you'll probably have to make two layers but try not to have loose rolls on top. Cut some of the garlic into fine slivers and crush the rest. Tuck the slivers in between the rolls here and there, then mix the crushed garlic with the lemon juice and tomato purée. Stir in about 150 ml (¼ pint) of warm water and pour over the *dolmas*, then lie a plate on top of them – inside the pan, to stop them moving around in the cooking. Cover the pan and simmer very gently for 1½–2 hours (fresh leaves will need the longer time), checking every 30 minutes or so and adding a little water as and when necessary. Pile onto a serving dish, with any liquid left in the pan poured over. Traditionally served hot – but leftovers are excellent cold.

Yalanci Dolmas

Stuffed Vine Leaves (Cold)

Nicknamed 'liar' *dolmas* since their stuffing contains no meat, these are glorious, with a spiced rice filling, cooked and cooled in a mixture of oil and lemon juice, to give a delicate contrast between the sweet and the tangy. In Persia, 50 g (2 oz) of raisins are usually added, and in Iraq we often used hazelnuts.

─────────◆─────────

Makes about 36 **dolmas**

45 large vine leaves
225 g (8 oz) long grain rice
1 large onion, skinned and finely chopped
50 g (2 oz) pine nuts or walnuts, finely chopped
1–2 large tomatoes, blanched, skinned and chopped
45–60 ml (3–4 tbsp) finely chopped parsley
30 ml (2 tbsp) dried mint or dill
freshly ground allspice
5 ml (1 tsp) ground cinnamon
Maldon or sea salt
freshly ground black pepper
3 large garlic cloves, skinned and finely chopped
175 ml (6 fl oz) olive oil
juice of 2 lemons
pinch of caster sugar

Wash and blanch fresh leaves in boiling water for a few minutes until soft, or soak packeted leaves in boiling water for 30 minutes, then drain and soak in cold water for another 5 minutes. Trim off the stalks and lay the leaves on a flat work surface, vein-sides upwards.

Wash the rice in boiling water, then rinse in cold, and drain thoroughly. Mix with the onion, nuts, tomatoes, herbs and spices then season – fairly highly – with salt and pepper. Stuff the leaves, rolling firmly but not too tightly to allow room for the rice to expand. Put a layer of leaves at the bottom of a large pan, and arrange the rolls in layers, side by side. Sprinkle over the chopped garlic, then mix the oil, lemon juice, sugar and about 150 ml (¼ pint) of warm water and pour over the *dolmas*. Tuck a small plate on top of the parcels, then cover the pan and simmer gently for 1½–2 hours until the leaves are quite tender. Add a little water from time to time as the liquid is absorbed. Cool, covered, in the pan, then pile onto a serving plate. These are often beautifully arranged in Turkey, in ever diminishing circles, with a slice of lemon tucked in between each *dolma*.

BAIDH

Eggs

Boil next the eggs, and smear them all in red;
With gold and silver let the *wast* be spread.
Now dust the lines with salt, yet not in haste,
But in appropriate measure, well to taste. [1]

E ggs have long held an established place in the Arab kitchen. It is said that the ancient Phoenicians ate ostrich, and even pelican's, eggs but more usual today are hen's eggs – plentiful all over the Middle East. They are believed to symbolise the mystery of life, since they form a circle without an opening and are often eaten at religious festivals, while egg dishes of one sort or another are nearly always served to break a fast. During the month-long fast of Ramadan, huge dishes of fried eggs and onions are prepared for the evening meal and the smell of the frying onions (which I adore) used to tantalisingly waft up to the verandah where I was trying to go to sleep on those hot summer nights. Even now, when I smell fried onions, I can see a dark blue sky, stars atwinkling, and hear the crickets competing with the harsh, gutteral sounds of excited Arabic greetings as the evening meal was being prepared.

For picnics – a favourite Arab past-time – hard-boiled eggs were a must. Wonderfully flavoured, and often coloured by long slow cooking with onion skins, sometimes coffee grounds too, they would then be dipped into a variety of spices and seasonings. Often they had been cooked the day before – buried in a stew so that the dish's flavours had filtered through the egg shells, to give a myriad tastes. This method is also used for eggs that are to accompany stews – the eggs being peeled, once hard-boiled, and returned to the pan for a final few minutes' cooking.

Another important picnic-basket ingredient were the *eggahs*, or *iggahs* – Arab omelettes or egg cakes, rather similar to the Spanish *tortilla*. Whether the Moors took them to Spain, or brought them home again, nobody quite knows but almost every country has their own variation while the Persians – as so often in the realm of cuisine – have made them a speciality. The Lebanese too have a rather nice refinement: instead of making one whole *eggah*, to be cut into wedges, most households have a special frying-pan with 10 or 12 circular depressions into which the egg mixture is poured, thus enabling the cook to make individual *eggahs* for a number of people at one time. The Turks tend not to mix their eggs into the vegetable, herb, or meat bases but just to break them on top of the cooked mixture, for poaching and serving whole. This is not to say that they are not a picnic food – in the Middle East, picnics are a very serious affair. The whole family is involved, a little stove is taken, often too a huge container with a stew or dish of beans, just needing reheating and, of course, the coffee pot.

Whatever the occasion, whatever the method of cooking, eggs are not merely our breakfast-time 'scrambled, fried, soft-or-hard-boiled?' They are exotically transformed with garlic, mint, lemon, vinegar, yogurt, onions, tomatoes – into dishes to be savoured and relished at all times.

Baidh Hamine
Hamine Eggs

This method of cooking eggs has been used all over the Middle East since time immemorial, and they are the traditional accompaniment to *Foul Medames* (page 94). Pale *café-au-lait* in colour with the yolks saffron-tinted and amazingly creamy in texture, people are inclined to disbelieve you when you tell them the eggs have been simmered for as long as six hours. If you have a solid fuel stove, you can leave them on top overnight. And if you are in a real hurry, you *can* cheat and simmer for only two hours – although the result is not quite so creamy, or chestnutty in taste.

SERVES 3–6
6 large eggs
the skins of 2–3 onions
coffee grounds (optional)
corn or olive oil

Put the eggs in a fairly deep saucepan into which they will fit quite snugly – if they have too much room to move around, you may find some of the shells splitting. I don't actually mind this since it gives a two-tone effect once the egg is completely peeled. Tuck the onion skins in between the eggs (the Turks often add some coffee grounds as well – this produces somewhat darker eggs) and then cover well with cold water. Spoon a layer of oil over the surface, to prevent the water from drying out, and cook, on the lowest possible heat for about six hours. Serve with *Foul Medames* (page 94) – lovely, too, dipped into fresh herbs.

Baidh bi Tom wa-Limoun
Fried Eggs with Lemon and Garlic

I had a young Palestinian nanny in Baghdad, whom I thought an angel. Unfortunately, she had a mother who was as demonic as I thought her daughter angelic. On her visits she used to terrify me and wage continual war with the cook, whom she was convinced was determined to poison her. Finally, his patience ran out and he refused to let her in the kitchen – or give her any food. Nothing daunted (and obviously well-prepared for this repeated ritual), she would set up her primus stove in a corner of the flat roof and for the rest of her stay, eat nothing but these eggs. Terror was over

come by curiosity – and the powerful aroma of frying garlic. I would creep upstairs and, sitting as far away as I decently could from that toothless old harridan, partake of the forbidden feast.

SERVES 6
40 g (1½ oz) unsalted butter
3 garlic cloves, skinned and finely chopped
30–45 ml (2–3 tbsp) lemon juice
6 eggs
15 ml (1 tbsp) cumin seeds
freshly ground white pepper
salt

Melt the butter in a large frying pan and when it's just bubbling, scatter in the garlic. Just as it's turning golden, stir in the lemon juice and then slide in the eggs. Fry them slowly for about 2 minutes until the yolks are just set. Quickly grind the cumin in a spice grinder and sprinkle over the eggs, then serve with a good grinding of white pepper and a sprinkling of salt.

Baidh Masluq
Hard-boiled Eggs with Cumin

These are a popular street snack in many countries of the Middle East – only the accompanying seasoning may vary. In Morocco they use cumin and salt; in Beirut I had them with cumin, salt and finely chopped fresh mint but I think my favourite was the Iraqi way with cumin and ground coriander – the sweetness of the coriander offsetting the bitter-sharp cumin.

SERVES 3–6
6 eggs, hard boiled
15 ml (1 tbsp) Maldon or sea salt
30 ml (2 tbsp) cumin seeds
15 ml (1 tbsp) coriander seeds

Peel the eggs and halve or quarter. Put the salt in a small bowl, lightly crush the cumin seeds in a mortar, and grind the coriander to a coarse powder in a spice grinder, then mix the spices thoroughly with the salt. Either sprinkle over the eggs or let people dip them into the mix.

Aijet Beythat
Fried, Spiced Hard-boiled Eggs

Another more refined version peels the hard-boiled eggs, then fries them in oil before rolling in spices. Dating from the medieval manuscript of al-Baghdadi, it uses coriander, cinnamon and cumin but when I was in Iraq they used cinnamon, cumin and tumeric – giving a mild curry flavour.

SERVES 3–6
6 eggs, hard boiled
olive oil, for frying
15 ml (1 tbsp) ground cinnamon
30 ml (2 tbsp) cumin seeds, lightly crushed
15 ml (1 tbsp) ground turmeric
15 ml (1 tbsp) Maldon or sea salt
coarsely ground white pepper

Peel the eggs and using a fine skewer (or large darning needle) prick them all over through to the yolks – this lets the flavours seep through the eggs and also helps to stop the whites splitting. Just cover the bottom of a small frying pan with a film of oil and heat until not quite smoking. Add the eggs and cook gently for about 5–6 minutes, turning frequently, until they are golden brown all over.

Mix all the spices together with the salt and a fairly generous grinding of white pepper, then roll the eggs in the mixture while they are still hot. Serve as a *meze* or with meat and vegetable stews.

Baidh ma' Na'na Muhammar
Deep-fried Eggs with Mint

This is a popular lunch, especially in small Arab villages.

SERVES 6
olive oil
6 eggs
fresh mint, finely chopped
fresh marjoram, finely chopped
12–18 spring onions, trimmed
Maldon or sea salt

Fill a large deep pan with the oil until it is about one-third full. Heat until not quite smoking. Break an egg in a saucer, and carefully slide into the pan, and then add the rest, one by one (this allows you to remove each one just as it sets – overcooking results in tough, leathery eggs).

Cook for about two minutes until the whites are slightly golden at the edges and the yolks just firm. Remove with a slotted spoon and put onto hot individual serving plates. Sprinkle generously with the mint and marjoram, put 2–3 spring onions on each plate, and scatter on a little salt. Serve at once with *Pitta* (page 98) and an assortment of pickles.

Baidh bi Gibne
Fried Eggs with Cheese

A popular dish all over the Middle East where it is usually served straight from the fire in the little double-handled frying-pan in which the eggs have been cooked. When making this dish for several people, I find it easier though to use one large frying pan. If you can't get the hard Greek cheeses, Kasseri, Kephalotiri or the less dry but firm Halumi, use slices of Labneh cheese – well dried out. Gruyère also makes a good substitute, as does a mature Cheddar.

SERVES 6
350 g (12 oz) hard cheese
30–45 ml (2–3 tbsp) olive oil or butter
6 eggs
Maldon or sea salt
freshly ground black pepper
cayenne pepper or ground cinnamon

Cut the cheese into six slices. Pour just enough oil to cover the surface of a frying pan large enough to hold the cheese slices snugly and heat until just smoking. Arrange the cheese in one layer and cook for a few minutes until it begins to melt at the edges and bubble, then quickly break an egg over each slice of cheese. Cook for another 2–3 minutes until the eggs are set to your liking. Sprinkle with salt, black pepper and a pinch of cayenne or ground cinnamon. Lightly cut through the whites and cheese with the edge of a fish slice, and serve at once. Some cooks also prick the yolks with a fine skewer to let them run out over the whites: unless cooking in individual portions, do this after putting the eggs on the plates.

Eggah bi Ful
Green Bean Egg Pie

Eggahs, or *iggahs*, are Arabian omelettes. Not the delicate, creamy, pan-to-table omelettes of the French kitchen, but a more solid egg pie omelette, crammed with vegetables, herbs, meat, brains – anything to hand really – and served cut in wedges like a cake. Ideal for the *meze* table and perfect for picnics and the pilgrimages which are a ritual of the many religious and national holidays, since they can be cooked and left to cool, or even reheated if wished. The sight of bands of pilgrims on their way to Mecca stopping by the wayside and warming up *eggahs* on their little primus stoves was not an uncommon one during my childhood. Nowadays, sophistication has set in and there are special charter flights to the Holy City. The form of travel may have changed. The diet has not, and in nearly every person's hand baggage will be a foiled-wrapped bundle – containing two or three *eggahs* to sustain them on the journey. This one was a favourite in Iraq, where green beans grew prolifically – and had to be picked every day, just as the sun was up, while they were still relatively small and tender. For by nightfall, they had almost doubled in size so fast was their growth rate. In Egypt fresh broad beans would be used instead.

SERVES 6
about 350 g (12 oz) fresh green beans, topped and tailed
6 eggs
salt and freshly ground black pepper
good pinch of turmeric
1–2 garlic cloves, skinned and finely chopped
30–45 ml (2–3 tbsp) finely chopped chervil
25–40 g (1–1½ oz) unsalted butter or oil

Cut the beans into 2.5 cm (1 inch) lengths, drop into a pan of boiling water and cook until just tender, about 5–15 minutes depending on the freshness and age of the beans. I wouldn't recommend using frozen beans – the texture is wrong, and the end result, to me at any rate, falls short of delicious. (This doesn't apply to broad beans – frozen are fine.) Drain and refresh under cold running water.

Beat the eggs in a large bowl, season with salt and pepper and a pinch of turmeric. Mix the garlic into the beans, then add the beans and chervil to the eggs. Melt the butter in a large frying-pan and just as it starts to sizzle, pour in the egg and bean mixture. Cover the pan and cook, slowly, for about 15–20 minutes until the eggs are set with just a thin film of liquid on top. If you are used to making *tortillas*, put a large plate on top of the pan and invert quickly, then return the omelette to the pan and cook, over a slightly higher heat, to brown the bottom. An easier method is to put the pan under a hot grill for 1 minute or so until nicely golden. Cut into wedges, or small pieces, and serve hot or cold.

Eggah bi Lahma
Meat Eggah

Meat *eggahs* are popular all over the Middle East. Lamb is the favoured meat but you can use beef as well. Again the vegetables and herbs vary according to what is in season, and from country to country.

SERVES 4–6
30 ml (2 tbsp) olive oil
1 large onion, skinned and finely chopped
2 garlic cloves, skinned and crushed
400 g (14 oz) minced lamb or beef
small handful fresh coriander leaves, finely chopped
5 ml (1 tsp) ground allspice
salt and freshly ground black pepper
6 large eggs
40–50 g (1½–2 oz) unsalted butter
To serve
a bowl of yogurt

Heat the oil in a frying pan, add the onion and sauté gently for 5 minutes until softened. Add the garlic and cook for another 2 minutes, then stir in the meat and fry until browned all over. Tip into a bowl, and stir in the coriander, allspice, salt and pepper. Beat the eggs until frothy, then blend into the meat.

Rinse and dry the frying pan and return to the heat. Melt the butter until just beginning to sizzle, then pour in the egg mixture and cook, covered, for about 20–25 minutes, slowly, until almost set. Pop under a very hot grill until golden on top. Accompany with a bowl of yogurt.

Yumurta Çilbir
Poached Eggs on Yogurt

A surprisingly good combination of eggs with yogurt from Turkey. Although always decorated with paprika in melted butter, the yogurt base often varies from family to family. Some add vinegar instead of lemon juice; some add neither. A little dried mint is liked by some cooks, a pinch of ground cumin by others. So please yourself: I sometimes like a touch of grated root ginger, and fresh tarragon is lovely in the summer.

SERVES 6

450 ml (¾ pint) natural yogurt
2–3 garlic cloves, skinned and finely chopped
Maldon or sea salt
juice of 1 lemon
10 ml (2 tsp) white wine vinegar
6 eggs
40 g (1½ oz) unsalted butter
good 15 ml (1 heaped tbsp) paprika

Beat the yogurt with the garlic cloves and a good pinch of salt, then whisk in the lemon juice and divide between six small bowls. Bring a large pan of water to the boil, and quickly dip in each egg, unshelled, for 20 seconds (hold in a ladle or sieve). This will help prevent the whites from running all over the place when you poach the eggs.

Bring another pan of water – preferably a wide shallow one, a sauteuse is ideal – to the boil. Whisk in the vinegar, then lower the eggs gently into the pan, not more than three at once, absolute maximum. Whatever anyone says poaching eggs is a fine art, which can very easily turn to disaster. If time is of the essence, then use two pans – but not an egg-poaching mould. The whites come out too thick, and besides, the eggs look as if they have come off a production line.

Let the water bubble once, then take the pan off the heat, cover and leave for 3–4 minutes, depending on how set you like your eggs. While they are setting, melt the butter in a small saucepan, when just beginning to sizzle, stir in the paprika. The butter should be tinged quite a deep red, so add a little extra paprika if need be.

Drain the eggs with a slotted spoon, put one into each bowl, and drizzle the butter over each egg in a zig-zag pattern.

Ajja
Onion Eggah

Another eggah which is popular in Iraq. In Egypt, leeks would probably be substituted, with the addition of a little lemon juice. In the Lebanon, courgettes are a favourite, sometimes with ground cinnamon or paprika added.

SERVES 4–6

2 large onions, skinned
small bunch of parsley, finely chopped
6 eggs
salt and freshly ground white pepper
pinch of ground ginger (optional)
45–60 ml (3–4 tbsp) olive oil

Either put the onions through a mincer or grate them (a food processor makes this simple), then mix with the parsley. Beat the eggs and add to the onions and parsley. Season with salt and a generous grinding of white pepper and add ginger if using (this is not strictly traditional, but our cook always used it – and I like the 'bite' it gives).

Heat the oil in a large frying pan, pour in the egg mixture and cook, covered, for about 20–25 minutes until firm. Either invert and return to the pan (in which case you may need the extra oil) or place under a hot grill to golden. Eat hot or cold.

Batata wa Tomatim Eggah
Potato and Tomato Eggah

The tomatoes we grew in Iraq were enormous – even bigger than beef steak tomatoes. Combined with potatoes and spring onions, they made this a favourite eggah. In Persia, they mash the potatoes, omit the tomatoes and add a bunch of finely chopped chives.

SERVES 4–6

50–60 g (2–2½ oz) unsalted butter
2 large potatoes, finely sliced
1 bunch spring onions, trimmed and chopped into rings
2 large beef steak tomatoes, finely sliced
3 large garlic cloves, skinned and crushed
6 cardamom pods
salt and freshly ground black pepper
6 large eggs
To garnish
45 ml (3 tbsp) finely chopped parsley

Melt 60 ml (4 tbsp) butter in a large frying pan, add the potatoes and gently fry for about 5 minutes on each side until softened. Add the remaining butter if necessary, then the onions, tomatoes and garlic. Mix everything together, then cook for another 10 minutes, stiring occasionally to prevent sticking.

Crush the cardamom pods, remove the seeds and pound in a pestle and mortar, then add to the pan and season with salt and freshly ground black pepper. Beat the eggs until frothy, then stir them into the pan, whisking around well. Cook slowly for about 15–20 minutes until nearly set, then place under a hot grill until golden. Sprinkle with the chopped parsley and serve cut into wedges.

Kuku Sabzy – I
Herb and Vegetable Egg Pie

The *kuku* or *kukuye* is the Persian version of the *eggah*. True to Persian perfection, it has been refined to great heights, particularly the herb and vegetable *kukus*, which traditionally appear on the New Year Table – the intense greenness symbolising new life in the year to come. *Kukus* are usually baked in the oven in a large rectangular dish, and make their appearance at almost every meal, cut into small squares as a *meze*, or into long, thin strips as a first course or side dish. The vegetables and herbs can be varied depending on what is in season – their freshness and greenness are the essence.

———————— ◆ ————————

SERVES 6 as a first course
225 g (8 oz) fresh spinach, or chard
3 thin leeks
1 small bunch spring onions
45 ml (3 tbsp) finely chopped parsley
30 ml (2 tbsp) of at least three of the following,
*   finely chopped:*
*   fresh coriander leaves*
*   fresh dill*
*   fresh tarragon*
*   fresh chives*
*   fresh chervil*
*   cos lettuce leaves*
salt and freshly ground black pepper
30 ml (2 tbsp) walnuts, chopped (optional)
8 eggs
40–50 g (1½–2 oz) unsalted butter
To serve
a bowl of yogurt

Wash and shake dry the spinach, then chop finely, discarding any thick stems. (Chard is popular in Persia but is hard to find in the West unless you grow it yourself – a sad lack, in my opinion.) Trim the leeks, and chop into thin rings. Do the same with the spring onions, using as much as possible of the green tops. Mix together the vegetables with all the herbs, season with salt and pepper then fold in the walnuts if using – they give an interesting texture.

Beat the eggs until frothy, then whisk into the herbs. Liberally grease an ovenproof dish and pour in the egg mixture. Bake in the oven at 180°C (350°F) mark 4, for 45 minutes to 1 hour, until firmly set. Cover the dish for the first 30 minutes, then remove the cover to allow the top to golden nicely. This is served both hot or cold, but always with a bowl of yogurt.

Kuku Sabzy – II
Walnut and Chive Egg Pie

A nuttier, yet more delicate, version of the traditional herb *kuku*, given to me by a Persian friend one New Year's Day in London. Do not be tempted to increase the saffron – too much will turn that delicate honey flavour into a bitter horror.

———————— ◆ ————————

SERVES 4
2 saffron strands
a good handful of chives, finely snipped
a good handful of parsley, finely chopped
45 ml (3 tbsp) fresh coriander leaves, finely
*   chopped*
25 g (1 oz) sultanas
50 g (2 oz) chopped walnuts
6 eggs
salt and freshly ground black pepper
25–40 g (1–1½ oz) unsalted butter

———————— ◆ ————————

Put the saffron strands into a small metal dish, then under a very hot grill for just under 1 minute. Crumble lightly, then pour over 15 ml (1 tbsp) boiling water and leave for 5 minutes. Mix together the herbs, sultanas and walnuts, then beat the eggs until frothy and whisk them in as well. Add the saffron and its water, season with salt and black pepper. Grease an ovenproof dish generously, pour in the eggs and cook, covered for the first 15–20 minutes, in the oven at 180°C (350°F) mark 4, for 30–40 minutes until set. Good hot or cold.

Kuku Bademjan
Aubergine Egg Pie

Also made as an *eggah* in other countries of the Middle East, where the tomatoes and saffron would be omitted.

———— ◆ ————

SERVES 4–6

2 medium aubergines
salt
2 strands saffron
45 ml (3 tbsp) olive oil
1 large tomato, finely sliced
1 small onion, skinned and finely chopped
1–2 garlic cloves, skinned and crushed
30 ml (2 tbsp) finely chopped dill
freshly ground black pepper
6 large eggs

———— ◆ ————

Cut the aubergines into chunks, put on a large plate and sprinkle liberally with salt. Leave for at least 30 minutes, then rinse under the cold tap to remove the bitter juices which will have risen to the surface of the aubergines. While they are standing heat the saffron strands under a hot grill, lightly crush, then cover with 15 ml (1 tbsp) of boiling water.

Heat the oil in a large frying pan, add the aubergines, tomato, onion and garlic cloves and sauté gently for about 5 minutes, then stir in the saffron, dill and season with salt and black pepper. Generously grease an ovenproof dish, mix the eggs into the vegetable mixture and pour into the dish. Cook for about 45 minutes, covered for the first 20 minutes, in the oven at 180°C (350°F) mark 4, until set. Leave to cool in the dish, then turn out and cut into small squares or long strips and serve with yogurt.

Ojja bil Merguez
Spicy Sausage Egg Pie

In Tunisia they add a highly spiced sausage and dried chillies to the *eggah*, and often stir the eggs until set – almost like rather firm scrambled eggs. You can also break the eggs whole in the centre of the pan, leaving the *merguez* sauce around the edges, but in this case you must eat the *ojja* hot. Substitute spicy Greek or Italian sausages if *merguez* is unobtainable. I have also used a *chorizo* (the spicy version) very successfully, but then add it with the eggs since it only needs heating up, not cooking.

———— ◆ ————

SERVES 4–6

45–60 ml (3–4 tbsp) olive oil
3 large garlic cloves, skinned and crushed
3 medium potatoes, cut into tiny dice
2–3 dried red chillies, seeded and coarsely chopped
30 ml (2 tbsp) tomato purée
15 ml (1 tbsp) caraway seeds
5 ml (1 tsp) Harissa (page 19)
5 ml (1 tsp) paprika
5–6 merguez (page 107), cut into thick slices
Maldon or sea salt
6 large eggs

———— ◆ ————

Fry the garlic for 1–2 minutes in the oil, then add the potatoes and the chopped chillies and gently fry for a further 10 minutes. Stir in the tomato purée, caraway, *Harissa* and paprika, then add water to just cover the mixture and stew slowly for about 30–40 minutes. Add the sausages and cook for another 15 minutes.

Beat the eggs, then pour into the pan, stirring to mix everything together. Then either continue stirring until firmly set but still creamy, or leave to set as if cooking an *eggah*. Serve hot if you have stirred the eggs, hot or cold if not.

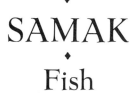

SAMAK
Fish

Here pungent garlic greets the eager sight
And whets with savour sharp the appetite,
While olives turn to shadowed night the day,
And salted fish in slices rims the tray.[1]

Cocktail parties were a source of endless fascination for me as a child. Firstly, of course there was the aura of mystery that hung over them, since I was obviously far too young to attend – and the forbidden is always fascinating. Secondly, there was the preparation, which always started the day before. In this I was allowed to partake. And here, I met my first fish in the Middle East. Strangely, although Iraq has two great, romantically historic rivers, the Euphrates and the Tigris, fish is not a favourite food – apart from *Masgouf*, the freshly smoked trout eaten with a hot, spicy sauce (page 46). What is popular though, and has been all over the Middle East since al-Baghdadi's time, is salt fish. The salting was once a necessity, in order to preserve the fish for a long time and over long distances: now it is loved and eaten for its own deliciousness. Whether our cook was consciously bringing to life al-Mu'tazz' poem, I doubt. Nonetheless, round silver platters of violet olives surrounded by the thinnest slivers of pale salt cod we did prepare. The mountain of olives was his domain; to me, fell the task of the surrounding sea. Paper-fine slices of soaked salt cod were poached in milk and garlic, of course, then cooled. I now had to arrange them in overlapping circles around the edges of the dishes. Then, with a quick flick of the tip of a knife, the exposed end of each slice was curled over to produce a pool of white wave crests, in the centre of which he would painstakingly build his dark tower. Oddly enough, I had completely forgotten this ritual until researching this book when I came across that poem – then it came suddenly flooding back. The pride in my beautiful 'seas', the holding of breath as he piled the olives higher and higher, and the rather wicked thoughts I occasionally had – almost willing them to come tumbling down. But he was far too professional for that.

However, it was not until we went to Beirut and Alexandria for holidays that I realised how much fish is, in fact, eaten in the Middle East. The Mediterranean abounds in wonderful varieties, and all are popular. None more so than the brightly coloured red mullet, *Sultan Ibrahim* to the Arabs, *barbounia* to the Turks and Greeks. Prepared in a multitude of ways, charcoal grilled, deep fried, wrapped in vine leaves, marinated, with various sauces, herbs and spices, or simply with garlic and lemon, you will, somehow, meet it in almost every country. Also abundant are the bigger grey mullet, a sea bream called *murgan* or *arous*, sea bass (*loukoz*), sole – quaintly named Moses' fish (*samak Moussa*), shad – considered a great delicacy in Morocco, mackerel (*uskumru*) beautifully stuffed in Turkey, sardines – boned and stuffed in Tunisia, swordfish – popular on skewers (*alla shish*), huge fresh tuna – baked in Morocco, tiny fresh anchovies – soused in Turkey (*hamsi bugulamsi*). Not to mention the more familiar cod, turbot, haddock, and a wonderful monster of a fish (unknown to us, but adored by the Syrians) called *sollar*, which is so repulsive that the poor creature is instantly beheaded on capture. In spite, or perhaps because, of this plethora or choice, most Middle Eastern recipes – and menus – merely state 'fish' (*samak*, *balik*, or *psari* depending exactly where you are) and local cooks will use whatever is to hand on the particular day they are cooking. Nonetheless, certain species lend themselves to certain dishes more readily than others. So, when substituting, you should pay attention not just to size but also to flavour and especially oiliness.

Within that small constraint, the world is your oyster. They, incidentally, were said to have been discovered by the Greeks but the ancients' enthusiasm for them is not shared by their descendants today. Turks on the other hand have always appreciated the delectable mollusc.

Mussels also find favour in Turkey, while Greeks and Turks share a love of shellfish, prawns, shrimps, and sweet succulent lobsters from the waters of the Bosphorous. That other strange family of sea creatures – the cephalopods – is most commended in Greece. Before the advent of package holidays to those enchanted isles, hardly a squid was to be seen on the fishmonger's slab. Now *kalamari* is a familiar dish, not just deep fried as a *meze*, but stewed in red wine, and dramatically stuffed. This last appears occasionally on Lebanese and Egyptian menus too, but elsewhere is not much found.

Kammounial Samak
Fish with Cumin

In Egypt and the Lebanon, cumin is often used to flavour fish – a surprisingly good marriage. I first had this dish in London, cooked by a Jordanian, brought up in Alexandria and Tripoli – and there are influences from all three countries in her recipe.

◆

SERVES 4–6

450 g (1 lb) fish heads and trimmings
1 small onion, skinned but left whole
1 bay leaf
6 black peppercorns
15 ml (1 tbsp) white wine vinegar or lemon juice
2–3 sprigs fresh parsley
900 g (2 lb) sea bass, grey mullet or any firm white fish
Maldon or sea salt
freshly ground black pepper
60–90 ml (4–6 tbsp) olive oil
2 large onions, skinned and finely chopped
1–2 garlic cloves, skinned and crushed
5 ml (1 tsp) cumin seeds, lightly crushed
7–8 sprigs fresh coriander leaves, finely chopped
juice of 1 lemon
cayenne pepper

◆

Put the fish trimmings into a large pan with the onion, bay leaf, peppercorns, vinegar and parsley. Add about 600 ml (1 pint) of cold water, bring to the boil, skim and simmer gently for about 45 minutes. Strain, then return the stock to the pan and reduce by rapid boiling to a generous 300 ml (½ pint).

Meanwhile, cut the fish into long, thickish strips, sprinkle with salt and pepper and leave for 30 minutes.

Heat 60 ml (4 tbsp) of the oil in a large frying pan, add the onions, garlic and cumin seeds and sauté gently for 10 minutes, until the onions are softened and the garlic and cumin begin to give out their aromas. Stir in the coriander leaves and cook for another 5 minutes, then remove with a slotted spoon and spread over the bottom of an ovenproof dish. Add the remaining oil to the pan, giving it 1–2 minutes to get hot, then fry the fish for about 4–5 minutes until golden all over. Drain and arrange on top of the onion mixture. Pour over the reserved fish stock, and cook in the oven, at 180°C (350°F) mark 4, for 10 minutes. Sprinkle with lemon juice and a good pinch of cayenne pepper and let it completely cool, in the dish, before serving. Nice with a rice salad, and particularly good with sesame seed bread.

Kilic Baligi Izgarasi
Grilled Swordfish Steaks

This elegant fish, so-named after its long, sword-like snout, is popular all over Turkey – in a variety of guises. For the *meze* table, I cut the steaks into small pieces, after cooking, but you could also chop them beforehand and thread them onto small skewers to make another Turkish favourite. Any firm, sweet, white fish may be substituted.

◆

SERVES 6

1 kg (2¼ lb) swordfish, in one piece
1 medium onion, skinned and grated, then squeezed to extract the juice
juice of 1 large lemon
15 ml (1 tbsp) olive oil
2 garlic cloves, skinned and crushed
15 ml (1 tbsp) coriander seeds, crushed
pinch of cayenne pepper
Maldon or sea salt
For the dressing
30 ml (2 tbsp) olive oil
30–45 ml (2–3 tbsp) lemon juice
30 ml (2 tbsp) finely chopped parsley
pinch of ground cinnamon

◆

Skin the fish – it is quite thick and pulls off easily, then cut into 6 thick steaks, and put these in a large, shallow dish. Mix together the onion and lemon juices, olive oil, garlic, coriander seeds and cayenne pepper, and pour over the fish. Leave to marinate for at least 3–4 hours, 5–6 if possible.

Just before cooking, sprinkle the fish with salt, then grill under a high heat for 4–6 minutes on each side until done right through. Cut the steaks into bite-sized pieces, arrange on a large dish, then mix the dressing ingredients together and pour over while the fish is still hot. Delicious served immediately but also good once cooled.

Sultan Ibrahim bi Tom
Red Mullet with Garlic

Crunchy, gleaming red mullet aromatic with garlic were a Beirut holiday treat. When I discovered a street stall in Cairo selling the same dish, using only the smallest fish, I was overjoyed. Room for this – and something else!

SERVES 6
90 ml (6 tbsp) finely chopped parsley
4 garlic cloves
Maldon or sea salt
freshly ground black pepper
6 small or medium red mullet, cleaned but livers left in
45 ml (3 tbsp) plain flour
olive oil, for deep frying
To serve
chopped parsley
lemon wedges

The livers are a great delicacy and contribute greatly to the wonderful smoky flavour. Mix the parsley with two of the garlic cloves, well crushed, then stuff about 15 ml (1 tbsp) of this into each fish. I find it easy to push it through the gills using a chopstick. Crush the remaining garlic with a good pinch or two of salt and a generous grinding of black pepper, then rub all over the skin of the fish.

Lightly sprinkle on both sides with flour, then heat a deep-fat frier with a good 5 cm (2 inches) of olive oil until beginning to smoke. Cook the fish in the deep-fat frier, not more than two at a time and then only if small, for 4–5 minutes until thoroughly crispy. Drain well, sprinkle with a little more parsley and serve with lemon wedges.

Barbounia sti-skara
Grilled Red Mullet

Simplicity itself, from Greece. Here the mullet are grilled, with frequent bastings of oil and lemon juice, then served sprinkled with parsley and chopped garlic, on a bed of thick, fresh tomato sauce. In other countries, the mullet may be fried, as in the previous recipe, or grilled, then served with a mayonnaise, tahina or walnut sauce. All are good – the difficulty is choosing.

SERVES 6
6 small or medium red mullet, cleaned but livers left in
Maldon or sea salt
freshly ground black pepper
90 ml (6 tbsp) olive oil
juice of 1 lemon
For the sauce
3 large beef steak tomatoes
pinch of granulated sugar
salt
15 ml (1 tbsp) olive oil
To garnish
2 garlic cloves, skinned and finely chopped
30–45 ml (2–3 tbsp) finely chopped parsley

Rub the fish on both sides with salt and plenty of black pepper, then leave for 15 minutes. Meanwhile, make the sauce: blanch the tomatoes, skin them and chop coarsely. Put in a pan, with a pinch of sugar and salt, then pour over the oil mixed with 45 ml (3 tbsp) of water. Stew them gently until soft but still holding their shape, about 5–7 minutes, then take off the heat.

Just before cooking, whisk together the oil and lemon juice then brush some over the fish. Grill for about 5 minutes on each side, under a high heat, and basting frequently, until nicely crispy. Reheat the sauce, if necessary, but do not let it boil. Arrange the fish on a platter with a little of the tomato sauce beside each one, then sprinkle with the chopped garlic and parsley. Good hot, scrumptious cold.

Samak Maqlu
Fried Fish

In modern day cookery, this title will encompass all kinds of fish, though more often than not red mullet, simply salted for 1 hour, then floured and fried in oil and served with a tahina or Pine Nut Tarator (page 16) and lemon wedges, of course. In al-Baghdadi's manual, it is a much more sophisticated affair: the challenge was irresistible. So too, I think, the end result – aromatically spiced and delicately coloured with saffron. After much experimenting, I think sole, or plaice fillets the best fish although it is good too with trout, the nearest relative to the Iraqi *shabbut*.

SERVES 6

12 fillets of sole or plaice
2–3 garlic cloves
Maldon or sea salt
2–3 sprigs thyme, leaves stripped off the stalks
5 ml (1 tsp) coriander seeds
5 ml (1 tsp) cumin seeds
2.5-cm (1-inch) piece cinnamon bark
2–3 strands saffron
5 ml (1 tsp) rose-water
5 ml (1 tsp) sesame oil
45 ml (3 tbsp) olive oil
lemon juice

———— ◆ ————

Cut the fillets crossways in two. Skin the garlic and crush it with about 2.5 ml (½ tsp) of salt, then pound with the thyme leaves until they are well crushed. Grind the coriander and cumin seeds with the cinnamon in a spice grinder until fine, then mix with the garlic and thyme. Spread some of the mixture over each fillet, then roll up and secure with a cocktail stick. Crumble the saffron, then stir the rose-water into 150 ml (¼ pint) boiling water, adding the saffron, and leave for 5 minutes.

Put the fillets into a frying pan, pour over the saffron water, and simmer gently for 5–10 minutes until the rolls are nicely coloured (turn them quite frequently) and most of the water has been absorbed. Drain and pat dry, discarding any liquid left in the pan.

Mix the sesame oil with the olive oil (al-Baghdadi uses only sesame oil for frying, but I find this too overpowering), heat, then add the fish rolls and fry for 3–4 minutes, again turning them all the time, until golden all over. Put on a serving dish, sprinkle with lemon juice and eat hot or cold – I prefer the latter. Cooling seems to enhance the delicacy of the flavours, yet makes them more definite.

Blehat Samak

Fish Sticks

These are popular all over the Middle East, with only the spices varying with the country. The Turks also have a delicious hot version, balik koftesi (fish balls), in which the mixture, once shaped, is lightly rolled in flour then fried in hot oil. Served without a sauce, just lots of lemon wedges and a sprinkling of parsley and cinnamon – very good.

SERVES 4–6

450 g (1 lb) fish heads and trimmings
1 small onion, skinned but left whole
few celery leaves
6 white peppercorns
2.5 ml (½ tsp) turmeric
900 g (2 lb) sea bream, bass, haddock, cod or
    halibut, skinned and filleted
3 slices white bread, crusts removed
1 medium onion, skinned and grated or minced
2–3 garlic cloves, skinned and crushed
Maldon or sea salt
freshly ground black pepper
45–60 ml (3–4 tbsp) finely chopped parsley or
    coriander leaves
5 ml (1 tsp) cumin seeds
5 ml (1 tsp) allspice or coriander seeds
1 large egg
plain flour
corn oil or other light oil, for deep frying
juice of 1 lemon or 2 limes
To garnish
chopped parsley

———— ◆ ————

Put the fish heads and trimmings into a large pan with the onion, celery leaves, peppercorns and turmeric. Add about 1 litre (1¾ pints) of cold water, bring to the boil, then simmer gently for about 25 minutes. Strain and reserve.

Put the fish through a mincer or whizz in a food processor. Soak the bread in cold water for 5 minutes, then squeeze, either mince or add to the fish and blend. Then add the onion, garlic, a generous seasoning of salt and black pepper and the parsley or coriander leaves. Grind the cumin seeds with either the allspice or coriander in a spice grinder, beat the egg lightly, then add the spices and egg to the fish and mix thoroughly. Take small lumps of the mixture and roll into small fingers. Sprinkle lightly with flour.

Heat about 2.5 cm (1 inch) of corn oil in a large pan until nearly smoking, then add a few rissoles and deep fry, turning occasionally, for 4–5 minutes until golden. Drain. Arrange in a clean pan, preferably wide and shallow, and pour over just enough of the reserved stock to cover the fish sticks. Squeeze in the lemon or lime juice, then bring to the boil quickly, lower the heat and simmer very gently for 15–20 minutes. Transfer the fish to a serving dish, pour over the sauce – which will set to a beautiful yellow jelly – and cool thoroughly. Serve, sprinkled with extra chopped parsley.

Tamara Keftedes
Fried Tamara Balls

Smoked cod's roe is not just reserved for *taramasalata* in Greece. It also makes its appearance in this delicious and unusual *meze*.

— ◆ —

SERVES 6–8
450 g (1 lb) smoked cod's roe
1 large onion, skinned and coarsely chopped
75–90 ml (5–6 tbsp) fresh white breadcrumbs
30 ml (2 tbsp) lemon juice
2–3 garlic cloves, skinned and crushed
freshly ground black pepper
15 ml (1 tbsp) finely chopped fresh marjoram
60 ml (4 tbsp) finely chopped parsley
2–3 egg whites (keep one in a separate bowl)
60–75 ml (4–5 tbsp) plain flour
olive oil, for deep frying
To serve
lemon wedges

— ◆ —

Skin the cod's roe, then chop coarsely, and mix with the onion, 75 ml (5 tbsp) breadcrumbs, lemon juice, garlic and herbs. Either put through a mincer or whizz in a food processor, in which case add two of the egg whites. (If mincing, add to the egg whites afterwards.) If the texture is too thin add the remaining breadcrumbs, if too thick, beat in the extra egg white, then chill for 2–3 hours – bear in mind that it will stiffen up with chilling.

Form into small balls or rissoles, keep your hands wet during this process, then roll lightly in flour. Heat a good 2.5 cm (1 inch) of oil in a pan until nearly smoking, then add the rissoles, not more than 4 or 5 at a time, and fry until crispy and golden. Drain and serve with lemon wedges.

Balik Pilakisi
Baked Fish

Any large fish, such as sea bream, bass, John Dory, halibut, cod or haddock is used for this Turkish dish, which is again served cold. In Greece, where it is called *psari plaki*, it is usually served hot (rather, warm – no food is ever served really hot), the potatoes are omitted and about 2.5 ml (½ tsp) of rigani is added.

SERVES 6
900 g (2 lb) filleted fish, cut into thick slices
1 large lemon
2 medium potatoes, finely sliced
2 large onions, skinned and finely sliced
3–4 garlic cloves, skinned and finely chopped
3 large tomatoes, blanched, skinned and sliced
small bunch of parsley, finely chopped
Maldon or sea salt
freshly ground black pepper
90 ml (6 tbsp) olive oil

— ◆ —

Arrange the fish in a large shallow baking dish. Peel the lemon (keep the zest for flavouring stocks and sauces) then cut into thin slices and lay on the fish. Cover with a layer of overlapping sliced potatoes, then strew on the onions. Scatter over the chopped garlic, then arrange the tomatoes on top and sprinkle thickly with the chopped parsley. Season, fairly highly, with salt and freshly ground black pepper, then mix the oil with about 300 ml (½ pint) of water. Pour over the dish – the liquid should just reach the layer of tomatoes, so if necessary, add a little more water.

Bake for 45 minutes to 1 hour in the oven at 180°C (350°F) mark 4. When a fork goes through to the bottom of the dish easily – it is ready. Remove and leave to cool to room temperature. For the *meze* table, I usually cut through this, in diamond shapes, for easy serving. A spoonful or two is particularly good tucked into a warm *Pitta* (page 98).

Uskumru Dolmasi
Stuffed Mackerel

One of the nicest facets of Middle Eastern cooking is how the simplest of ingredients are transformed into magnificent dishes. This is one of the most spectacular when, for festive occasions, the flesh of the mackerel is squeezed out of the fish, boned, then mixed with a spicy nut and onion stuffing and returned to the fish skins. For less brave souls, I give a somewhat easier version below but I am assured by Turkish friends that the process is not complicated – you merely need confidence. One good tip I received was to skin the fish rather than squeeze out the flesh: cut off the head, rub the fish roughly between your hands, then turn down the top centimetre (½ inch) of skin nearest the head and pull on the backbone (which is now visible) ripping it out and pulling off the skin simultaneously. I shall try – one day.

SERVES 6
For the stuffing
3 medium onions, skinned and finely chopped
30 ml (2 tbsp) olive oil
75 g (3 oz) chopped walnuts
50 g (2 oz) hazelnuts
25 g (1 oz) pine nuts
50 g (2 oz) sultanas
Maldon or sea salt
freshly ground black pepper
2.5 ml (½ tsp) ground allspice
2.5 ml (½ tsp) ground cinnamon
10 ml (2 tsp) dried dill
60 ml (4 tbsp) finely chopped parsley
For the fish
6 small mackerel, cleaned but left whole
2 large eggs, beaten
40 g (1½ oz) dry, fine white breadcrumbs
90 ml (6 tbsp) olive oil
To serve
lemon wedges

First make the stuffing: fry the onions gently in the olive oil until soft and golden. Put the walnuts and hazelnuts into a grinder and grind coarsely – you want a certain amount of grittiness to contrast with the soft flesh of the fish. Add the nuts to the onions, then add the pine nuts, sultanas and a generous seasoning of salt and pepper and cook for a further 5–7 minutes. Stir in the spices and herbs, mixing well.

Wash the mackerel, running cold water through them to remove any blood, then dry thoroughly. Divide the stuffing mixture into 6, and stuff into each fish. Either secure the openings with cocktail sticks or sew up (I find it easier to cook the fish if they are sewn but *en famille* I confess to using sticks), then dip the fish first in the beaten eggs, then in breadcrumbs, coating well.

Heat 30 ml (2 tbsp) of the olive oil in a large frying pan, add no more than 2 fish at a time (you probably won't be able to anyway) and fry for 4 minutes on each side until crispy. Drain, and cook the rest of the fish in the same way. Can be eaten straight away but I think even better when allowed to cool, cut into thick slices and served with lemon wedges.

Uskumru Papaz Yahnisi
Cold Mackerel

A famous Turkish speciality and, I think, a particularly good way of cooking mackerel, its sometimes rather strong taste being softened by the vegetables. Variations are also cooked using swordfish, cut in thick slices, or whole red mullet.

SERVES 6
1 large mackerel, weighing 900 g–1.4 kg (2–3 lb)
60 ml (4 tbsp) olive oil
2 large onions, skinned and finely sliced
1 green pepper, finely sliced
3–4 garlic cloves, skinned and finely chopped
3 large tomatoes, blanched, skinned and thickly sliced
90 ml (6 tbsp) finely chopped parsley
15–30 ml (1–2 tbsp) tomato purée
pinch of granulated sugar
Maldon or sea salt
freshly ground black pepper
juice of 1–2 lemons
50 g (2 oz) small black olives, stoned

Have the fish cleaned but leave it whole, just making a few scores on either side with a sharp knife. Heat the oil in a large frying pan, then sauté the fish on both sides for about 3–4 minutes until nicely browned and remove from the pan. Add the onions and cook until softened and lightly coloured – about 10 minutes, then add the pepper and garlic and fry for a further 5 minutes. Put the tomatoes in the pan, scatter over the parsley, then mix the tomato purée and sugar with about 150 ml (¼ pint) of water and pour over. Season with salt and pepper, bring to a bubble, then simmer for 10–15 minutes. Gently lay the fish on top, then push down carefully to cover it with the sauce and cook for another 10 minutes, spooning over a little sauce after 5 minutes if necessary. Transfer to a serving dish, squeeze over the juice of 1–2 lemons and scatter on the olives. Leave to cool completely, then cut into thick slices.

Yakhnit Samak Harrak
Cold Fish with Paprika

The Lebanese version of a dish found throughout the Middle East, where cold fish dishes are much appreciated – an appreciation that I think we in the West should learn to share. Apart from the ubiquitous salmon in aspic, we almost completely ignore this delicious and versatile aspect of fish cookery.

◆

SERVES 4–6
900 g (2 lb) sea bass, cod or haddock, filleted
Maldon or sea salt
the head and trimmings of the fish
60–75 ml (4–5 tbsp) olive oil
2 large onions, skinned and finely sliced
2–4 garlic cloves, skinned and finely chopped
5 ml (1 tsp) paprika
5 ml (1 tsp) ground cinnamon
1.5–2.5 ml (¼–½ tsp) cayenne pepper
2.5 ml (½ tsp) caraway seeds, lightly crushed
juice of 1–2 lemons

◆

Rub the fish with salt on both sides, then leave to stand for 1 hour. Make a stock with the fish trimmings and a scant 600 ml (1 pint) of cold water, then strain and reserve. Heat the oil in a frying pan, add the fish and fry on both sides until golden, about 5–6 minutes. Remove from the pan, add the onions and fry for 5 minutes until softened, then add the garlic and cook for 10 minutes until golden. Drain off all the oil, arrange the fish on top of the onions, sprinkle over the spices (use even less cayenne if you don't like things hot!) and the juice of 1 lemon, then pour on enough fish stock to come level with the fish. Bring to the boil, then simmer gently for 15–20 minutes. Remove from the heat, sprinkle over more lemon juice if you think it needs it (I like it lemony) and a little salt. Cool to room temperature before serving with hot, soft Pittas (page 98).

Samak Maschwi
Roasted Fish

This is a dish for joyous occasions – always a large gathering. Particularly popular in Syria, Egypt and the Lebanon – and ideal for the centre of the meze table. Smaller fish also are baked in the same way, then dressed with oil, lemon juice and parsley, whisked together.

SERVES 8–12
1.8 kg (4 lb) sea bass, bream or grey mullet, cleaned but left whole (see also below)
Maldon or sea salt
freshly ground black pepper
60–90 ml (4–6 tbsp) olive oil
1 lettuce, shredded
To garnish
black and green olives, stoned
lemons, sliced
parsley sprigs
whole radishes
strips of red and green peppers
sliced pickled cucumbers
fried almonds and/or pine nuts

◆

Traditional recipes for this always instruct you to remove the eyes. If you are squeamish, get your fishmonger to do this for you when he's cleaning it. Rinse the fish, then rub all over with salt and chill for 30 minutes. Bring back to room temperature, then rub with lots of black pepper, and olive oil. Brush a large piece of thick foil with oil, then lay the fish on it, wrap and seal well. Bake in the oven at 180°C (350°F) mark 4. Check after 1 hour – if the fish is firm and opaque yet flakes easily, it's done. Otherwise give it another 10–15 minutes but take care not to overcook it. Carefully transfer onto a huge serving dish lined with the shredded lettuce, then garnish decoratively in an eastern pattern, using stars, crescents and criss-cross lines. Olives, lemon slices and parsley sprigs are a must – from the rest, choose two or three or all. Serve cold with bowls of mayonnaise – preferably garlicky, and Consbareyah (page 16).

Sardinát Muhnnat
Stuffed Sardines

In much of the Middle East, fish is endowed with magical omens, particularly so in Tunisia, where it is almost a national symbol, beautifully painted on houses, crockery and materials. Even jewellery is fashioned from the fish. One of the most beautiful bracelets I bought in Tunis consists of 14 little fish, delicately outlined in pure gold filigree, linked to lie side by side encircling the wrist.

Newly wed couples traditionally walk over a large fish to ensure marital happiness, while in Egypt a new home will be blessed with a first meal of fish – which delighted my grandfather, who moved often and adored fish, in all its forms. Even in far away Persia, not a great fish eating nation (though they have some of the finest caviar in the world) New Year's Eve is nearly always celebrated with a fish dish – to purify oneself and bring luck in the year to come.

These stuffed sardines, a Tunisian speciality, always remind me of that beautiful country – and the bracelets I left behind.

━━━━ ◆ ━━━━

SERVES 6
12 fresh sardines
15 ml (1 tbsp) olive oil
1 onion, skinned and finely chopped
small bunch of parsley, very finely chopped
15 ml (1 tbsp) cumin seeds, crushed
3–4 garlic cloves, skinned and crushed
1.5 ml (¼ tsp) cayenne pepper
Maldon or sea salt
freshly ground black pepper
2 large eggs, beaten
homemade dried finely crushed white breadcrumbs, for coating
oil, for deep frying
To serve
lemon wedges

━━━━ ◆ ━━━━

Cut off the heads and tails of the sardines, then wash and slip out the backbones. Heat the oil, add the onion and cook, gently, for 10–15 minutes until very soft and lightly golden. Add the parsley, cumin, garlic, cayenne and a good seasoning of salt and black pepper, and fry for another 3–4 minutes, mixing well. Tip into a bowl and moisten with about 15 ml (1 tbsp) of the beaten eggs, then spread a little down the middle of each sardine. Skewer them together with cocktail sticks, threading them in and out to ensure the stuffing doesn't fall out.

Dip the fish in the eggs, then roll well in the breadcrumbs, pressing them lightly on with your fingertips.

Heat a good 5 cm (2 inches) of oil in a wide, deep pan. When just smoking, add 2 sardines and cook for about 5–6 minutes, turning once, until nicely browned and crispy. Drain, cook the remaining fish, and serve with lemon wedges. Also very good cold.

Hamsi Bugulamsi
Soused Anchovies

Anchovies, in any form, I have always adored, so this Turkish dish is a great favourite. Small sardines make an ideal substitute when fresh anchovies are unobtainable (which is nearly always) but there are two fishmongers in London who do sometimes have these wee fish – and then it's not just the pussies who are purring! Both anchovies and sardines, as well as red mullet, are also often wrapped in vine leaves and simply grilled. Excellent.

━━━━ ◆ ━━━━

SERVES 6
1 kg (2¼ lb) fresh anchovies or sardines, as small as possible
120 ml (8 tbsp) olive oil
pinch of Maldon or sea salt
30 ml (2 tbsp) finely chopped fresh dill
2.5 ml (½ tsp) dried dill seed
45 ml (3 tbsp) finely chopped parsley
freshly ground black pepper (optional)
1.5 ml (¼ tsp) ground cinnamon (optional)
juice of 1–1½ lemons

━━━━ ◆ ━━━━

Make a small slit in the belly of each anchovy, then slip a knife in and tweak out the innards (this is a bit fiddly but I think it's worth it – with sardines I don't bother, as I like the rather musky flavour, but many people don't). Wash quickly under cold water, then pat dry. Arrange the fish, side by side, head to tail, preferably in one layer either in a large frying pan or in a baking tin if you haven't a large enough frying pan, then pour over the oil and a sprinkling of salt (I mean a sprinkling), then add about 300 ml (½ pint) of cold water, the dill and dill seed, parsley, pepper and cinnamon, if using (these last seasonings vary from region to region). Cover the pan, bring gently to the boil and simmer for 7–8 minutes. Take off the heat, sprinkle over the juice of 1 lemon, then leave to cool. Check if the sauce needs a little more lemon juice, adding if necessary, then serve with warm, crusty sesame bread – to mop up the juices. Lovely for *meze* – even better for supper.

Masgouf

Fresh Smoked Fish with Curried Pepper Sauce

The speciality for which Iraq is famous. As night falls on the shores of the River Tigris, the sparkle of little fires lights up the black sky – a glittering necklace of beacons as far as the eye can see. Cries of triumph echo up and down the banks as the fish are caught – Tigris Salmon we called it, in fact a type of large trout known as *shabbut* to the Arabs. Split down the belly, held open by thin skewers of thorn bush, they were then hung around the fire, flesh inwards to absorb the smoke, skins outwards gleaming silver in the moonshine. On the fire beneath, were huge pans of sizzling onion and tomatoes, hotly peppered and aromatically spiced, waiting for the fish to be almost smoked, when they would be laid on the ashes, skin-side down, and spread with the fiery sauce. A few nicks with a knife tip to let the sauce permeate the sweet flesh then, when the skin was charred and blistered, they were ready. And so were we.

It is impossible to reproduce this dish far away from that fabled river. The best approximation I ever achieved was by half-cooking fresh trout over a smoking barbecue then, when the smoke had died down and the coals were glowing, I finished their cooking by grilling them – covered in sauce – on the grid. Reminiscent of a dish my mother often made – simplicity itself.

———————— ◆ ————————

SERVES 6

6 small trout or 6 cod steaks
30 ml (2 tbsp) coriander seeds
15 ml (1 tbsp) white peppercorns
2.5 ml (½ tsp) Maldon or sea salt
6 cardamom pods, husks removed
5 ml (1 tsp) cumin seeds
1.5 ml (¼ tsp) fenugreek seeds
2.5-cm (1-inch) piece fresh root ginger, peeled and
  sliced
2.5-cm (1-inch) piece cinnamon bark
2–3 large onions, skinned and finely sliced
3 large tomatoes, blanched, skinned and finely
  sliced
90 ml (6 tbsp) olive oil
juice of 2 lemons
3–4 garlic cloves, skinned and finely chopped
To garnish
fresh coriander leaves, finely chopped

If using trout, split them open, clean and wash but leave the heads and tails on. Cod steaks merely need a quick rinse. Put all the spices, except the ginger and cinnamon bark, into a spice grinder and grind until fine, then add the ginger and cinnamon and grind again. Rub the mixture over the fish – on the flesh side only with the trout, both sides for cod, and leave to stand for 30 minutes.

Lightly grease a large baking dish, then arrange the fish side by side. Cover each with a layer of onion, then tomatoes. Mix the oil and lemon juice with about 90 ml (6 tbsp) of water and pour over the fish, then scatter on the garlic. Bake in the oven, at 180°C (350°F) mark 4, for 45 minutes to 1 hour, until the fish is done. Sprinkle with finely chopped coriander leaves and serve hot or cold.

Loukhoz Harrah

Hot Spiced Bass

In the Lebanon, bass is a favourite fish, especially for large gatherings when it is always served whole. This dish, with its fiery sauce of Yemeni origin, I remember having at a picnic in the hills overlooking Beirut. I can still recall being incredulous at the thought of those snow-capped mountains with people skiing, while down below the beaches were crowded with tiny figures, sunbathing and swimming – a mere hour separating the two scenes.

———————— ◆ ————————

SERVES 6–8

900 g–1.4 kg (2–3 lb) sea bass, cleaned but left
  whole
1 medium onion, skinned and grated or minced
4 garlic cloves, skinned and crushed
2.5 ml (½ tsp) Maldon or sea salt
15 ml (1 tbsp) paprika
1.5 ml (¼ tsp) cayenne pepper
1.5 ml (¼ tsp) fenugreek seeds, crushed
2.5 ml (½ tbsp) cumin seeds, crushed
small bunch fresh parsley, finely chopped
handful fresh coriander or celery leaves, finely
  chopped
150 ml (¼ pint) olive oil
juice of 2 lemons
To serve
lemon juice

Wash the fish, and score two or three times on both sides. Mix the onion and garlic with the seasonings, including parsley and coriander or celery, then whisk in the olive oil and lemon juice until you have a thick pasty sauce. Alternatively, whizz everything together in a blender, then coat the fish thickly with the paste, on one side. Grill, under a medium heat for 15–20 minutes, brushing with a little more oil if necessary, then turn over, coat the other side with more of the paste and cook for another 20–25 minutes – again basting with more oil if need be. When the fish flakes easily and the skin is deeply golden and crispy, it is done. Cut into thick slices, sprinkle with a little more lemon juice and serve hot or cold.

Bakaliaros Skorthalia
Salt Cod Fritters with Garlic Sauce

Having rediscovered salt cod, which can be a problem to find in England, therefore when I did, I bought large quantities, I had to experiment with it all ways. These Greek fritters, supremely simple, are also exquisitely more-ish.

———— ♦ ————

SERVES 4–6
700 g (1½ lb) salt cod
For the batter
100 g (4 oz) plain flour
good pinch of Maldon or sea salt
15 ml (1 tbsp) olive oil
1 egg white
olive oil, for frying
To serve
Skorthalia Sauce (page 15)
lemon wedges
radishes

———— ♦ ————

Soak the salt cod in cold water for 24 hours, changing the water frequently. Or, leave under cold running water for about 12 hours. Then strip off the skin and bone. Cut into large cubes – about 5 cm (2 inches) square.

To make the batter: sift the flour with the salt, pour over the oil and a good 150 ml (¼ pint) of tepid water and whisk together thoroughly. Leave to stand for 1 hour at room temperature – do not chill. Just before cooking, whisk again, then beat the egg white until stiff peaks form and fold into the batter. Dip the pieces of fish into the batter while heating enough oil in a large pan to deep fry. When it is nearly smoking, add a few cubes of fish, and fry quickly until golden all over, about 5 minutes. Drain

and cook the rest. Serve with Skorthalia Sauce (page 15), lemon wedges and – traditionally – a plate of radishes.

Malih bi-Laban
Salt Fish in Milk

I was delighted to find this recipe in al-Baghdadi, so reminiscent of our 'hat party' platters. I think, though, that our cook must have eliminated the initial frying since his fish was always milky-white. And yet, when I did that the flavour was not quite right. No matter, the golden cubes (easier than fine slices) are enticing – especially with a mound of pale green olives – and the taste perfect. A good introduction to those who are under the impression that they abhor salt fish.

———— ♦ ————

SERVES 4–6
700 g (1½ lb) salt cod
olive oil, for deep frying
about 150 ml (¼ pint) milk
2 garlic cloves, skinned and crushed
freshly ground black pepper
2.5 ml (½ tsp) coriander seeds
2.5 ml (½ tsp) cumin seeds
1-cm (½-inch) piece cinnamon bark
To serve
lime wedges (optional)

———— ♦ ————

Soak the cod in cold water for at least 24 hours, changing the water every 2–3 hours. Even better, if you can organise it, is to leave the fish under a running tap for 12–14 hours. Put into a large pan, well covered with fresh water and bring to the boil, then simmer for 25–30 minutes. Drain the fish, cool until easy to handle, then skin and bone. Cut into ¾-inch cubes. Heat a good 2.5 cm (1 inch) of olive oil in a large pan until nearly smoking, then add 6–8 pieces of fish and fry, turning over once or twice, until golden. This will take 2–3 minutes: don't be tempted to put too much fish in at one time or the temperature of the oil will drop and the fish will be soggy. When all the fish has been fried, put in a large shallow pan and just cover with milk. Stir in the garlic and a generous amount of freshly ground black pepper and simmer for about 12–15 minutes until the milk has all but disappeared. Put on a serving dish. Grind the coriander, cumin and cinnamon until very fine, sprinkle over the fish, and leave to cool. I particularly like this with a little fresh lime juice sprinkled over.

Kalamari
Grilled Squid

Squid is one of the prizes of the Mediterranean, much unappreciated elsewhere except in Japan. In Greece, Turkey and Cyprus though they have long realised its excellence, nowhere more so than in this excellent, and simple, *meze*. Very tiny squid, *kalamarakia*, which I like for this dish, are, in Greece, more usually dipped in batter, deep fried and served with lemon wedges, while the larger squid are popular, in Cyprus, stewed in red or white wine, then left to cool before serving.

———————— ◆ ————————

Serves 6–8
1.4 kg (3 lb) squid
Maldon or sea salt
freshly ground black pepper
15–30 ml (1–2 tbsp) finely chopped fresh
   marjoram
90 ml (6 tbsp) olive oil
juice of 1 large lemon
2–3 garlic cloves, skinned and finely chopped

———————— ◆ ————————

To clean the squid, stretch out the tentacles away from the body, grip them and pull hard. The head and insides of the squid will come cleanly away. Cut off the tentacles just above the head – keeping them, discarding the rest, including the ink sac. Slip the nib-like transparent bone out of the body, then rinse the body in cold running water – inside and out, rubbing off the pale pink thin membrane. Wash the tentacles. You will now have a pale translucent body with two little flaps (perfectly edible) and rose-coloured tentacles ready for cooking. The whole operation only takes 1–2 minutes, so don't be daunted.

Chop the body and tentacles into small rings and arrange on a grill pan with the grid removed. Sprinkle with salt, pepper and marjoram. Mix together the oil, lemon juice and chopped garlic and pour over. Grill, under a high heat, for 15–20 minutes until tender. Then serve, with the pan juices poured over – and crusty bread to mop them up.

Kalamaria Kathista
Squid Stewed in Wine

Another squid favourite, particularly in Cyprus. Either red or white wine may be used – I prefer white for appearances' sake, but red gives a lovely gutsy flavour.

Serves 4–6
1.4 kg (3 lb) squid
60 ml (4 tbsp) olive oil
2–3 large onions, skinned and finely chopped
2–3 garlic cloves, skinned and crushed
Maldon or sea salt
freshly ground black pepper
2.5-cm (1-inch) piece cinnamon bark
pinch of granulated sugar
300 ml (½ pint) dry white, or red, wine
45–60 ml (3–4 tbsp) finely chopped parsley

———————— ◆ ————————

Clean the squid by pulling on the tentacles, then cut off just above the head, discarding the head and innards. Wash the body inside and out, and pull away the pinkish outer membrane. Rinse the tentacles. Chop everything into small rings.

Heat the olive oil, add the onions and fry gently for about 5 minutes. Add the squid and garlic and cook for a further 10 minutes until the onions are softened. Season, then add the cinnamon bark, sugar and wine. Bring to the boil, lower the heat and half cover the pan. Simmer gently for about 1 hour until the squid is quite tender and most of the liquid has been absorbed. Pile on a serving dish, with the pan juices poured over. Sprinkle on the parsley and cool to room temperature before serving.

Kırmızı Biberli Istakoz
Lobster in Paprika Oil

The prize of the Bosphorous is its lobster. Delicately sweet and succulent, and perfectly set off in this simple paprika oil dressing.

———————— ◆ ————————

SERVES 4–6
2 lobsters, preferably hen, each weighing about
   700 g (1½ lb)
175 g (6 oz) salt (optional)
175 ml (6 fl oz) olive oil
15–30 ml (1–2 tbsp) paprika
Maldon or sea salt
juice of 1 large lemon
To serve
finely chopped parsley
lemon juice

———————— ◆ ————————

If the lobsters are live, bring about 2.3 litres (4 pints) of water to the boil, add the salt, then when rapidly boiling again, plunge the lobsters in, head first, then cook for about 15 minutes until bright red and the tail flesh is opaque. Take out of the pan and cool, lying the lobsters on their back so that a little of the liquid is retained in the shell, keeping the flesh succulent.

When cool, or if bought ready-cooked from the fishmonger, split the lobsters in two down the middle with a heavy cleaver – have the lobsters, shell side up, with their heads facing away from you. Then cut off and crack the claws with a sharp blow – keep these to a minimum, you want to be able to extract the flesh but not have too much cracked shell. Remove the little bag visible in the lobster's head – this is the stomach and must be discarded. Then pull out the long thin black vein running from the head to the tail. Now, all that is left which is inedible are the feathery gills which lie between the creamy coloured head meat and the small legs – these should be removed after scraping out the head meat and the liver (or tomally) which is greenish in colour and a great delicacy. The soft pale pink meat under the gills is also edible. All the rest of the flesh (and the coral or roe, if there is any) can now easily be taken out. Cut the large tail meat into pieces, then extract the sweet claw flesh. Mix all the meat together in a large shallow bowl, then whisk the oil with the paprika and a little salt and pour over the lobsters. Sprinkle with the juice of 1 lemon, and leave for 1 hour, turning the meat occasionally. Serve sprinkled with finely chopped parsley and extra lemon juice if you wish. Exquisitely simple but deceptively rich, so rice, or bread, and a plain salad should be the only accompaniments.

Midye Tavasi
Deep Fried Mussels

Istanbul, that most exotic of Eastern cities, boasts a glorious fish market. Here, on the wharf side, where the Bosphorous comes to greet the Golden Horn, are dozens of makeshift restaurants. Small tables and wooden benches are set out on the quay, curtained off from the neighbouring competitors by large sails. Within minutes of sitting down, you are presented with a huge platter of freshly fried fish, warm bread, and a cool cucumber salad. Each stall has its own speciality – these mussels are one of my favourites. A pint of mussels, incidentally, is equivalent to 450 g (1 lb).

SERVES 6–8
For the batter
1 large egg
225 g (8 oz) plain flour
For the mussels
36 large mussels, about 3 pints
Maldon or sea salt
plain flour
olive oil, for deep frying
lemon juice

Make the batter first, by whisking the egg until frothy, then beating in 300 ml (½ pint) of water, and gradually sifting in the flour, beating all the time. Leave to stand for 1 hour.

This gives you plenty of time to prepare the mussels. Nowadays, they can often be bought already cleaned, in which case I find a quick rinse in cold water, simply pulling on the little beard which protrudes from each shell, and discarding it, is enough. If they have not already been cleaned, you will have to scrub each one, under cold running water, to remove any barnacles, seaweed and, of course, the beards. Either way, any mussels that do not close quickly when tapped sharply should be thrown away, as should any that are broken or feel inordinately heavy for their size (these will probably be full of mud which will ruin the dish). Once the water is continually clear, with no sand or grit floating in it, the mussels are ready. Put them into a very large saucepan, pour over about 150 ml (¼ pint) of water and sprinkle with salt. Cover the pan and cook over a very high heat for about 5–7 minutes, shaking the pan every now and again. Once the mussels are opened, they can be removed from the pan (you can do this in batches if you like). Discard any that do not open. Drain them on a clean tea towel and take out of their shells. All this can be done 2–3 hours in advance of the final cooking, but do not refrigerate the mussels or they will toughen.

Just before cooking, whisk the batter once more, roll the mussels lightly in the flour, then dip into the batter. Heat the oil in a deep fat fryer or large saucepan, when it just begins to smoke carefully drop a few mussels 5–6 at once, no more, and cook for 1 minute, until golden and puffed up. Drain, cook the rest the same way, then serve, sprinkled with lemon juice and accompanied by *Teradot* (page 17) and a cucumber salad.

Midye Dolmasi
Stuffed Mussels

If you walk on down the quayside towards the Galata Bridge, where old and new Istanbul meet, and where the painted fishing boats are tied up – their hauls haggled over, with much shouting, squeezing and prodding, all 'in the name of Allah', you will come to the more elegant – and expensive – fish restaurants. Wonderfully decorated with intricately patterned tiles and fretwork, you can sit here, gaze out on the ever-changing sea panorama, and dine on huge prawns, sweet lobsters, and these glorious stuffed mussels. Like many good things in life, they need time, for the preparation is fiddly. But the consolation is that they can be completed several hours ahead of serving.

Serves 6–8
36 large mussels, about 3 pints
30 ml (2 tbsp) olive oil
1 large onion, skinned and grated or minced
50 g (2 oz) pine nuts
2 small tomatoes, blanched, skinned, seeded and finely chopped
50 g (2 oz) currants
45 ml (3 tbsp) finely chopped parsley
5 ml (1 tsp) granulated sugar
5 ml (1 tsp) ground allspice
5 ml (1 tsp) finely chopped fresh dill
Maldon or sea salt
freshly ground black pepper
50 g (2 oz) long grain rice
150 ml (¼ pint) fish stock
To serve
finely chopped parsley (optional)
lemon wedges

Clean the mussels, scrubbing them if necessary, then pull off the beards and leave them to soak in fresh cold water. Heat the oil, add the onion and sauté for 3–4 minutes until softened. Add the pine nuts, tomatoes, currants, parsley, sugar and spices and cook for another 2 minutes. Then season fairly highly with salt and black pepper, add the rice and stir until all the grains are gleaming. Pour in the stock, or you can use water, bring to the boil, then simmer gently for about 10–15 minutes until the rice is almost cooked and the liquid absorbed. Cool this stuffing mixture.

Now, for the tricky bit. Put the mussels in a large bowl of cold water, have ready a clean large pan, some cotton and scissors. Using an oyster knife, or a stout, thick-bladed knife, force open each mussel slightly, loosening but not separating the two shells. I find the easiest way to do this, is to pick out a mussel from the bowl that is already slightly open – even inserting the knife blade between the shells before taking out of the water. That way, even if the mussel tries to shut immediately, at least the knife is in! Over the pan, force it open – any juices can then fall into the pan. Put a scant 5 ml (1 tsp) of stuffing into each mussel, then close the shell and tie with string. Arrange in the pan, side by side, making close-fitting layers. Add enough boiling water to just cover the mussels and simmer for about 15 minutes. Remove from the pan, arrange on a serving dish and cool to room temperature. Just before serving, snip the cotton, sprinkle with a little more chopped parsley if wished, and have plenty of lemon wedges. Very, very good.

Samak Kebab
Fish Kebabs

Popular in Alexandria are these little sticks of *samak kebab*.

Serves 6
900 g (2 lb) sea bass, bream, cod, turbot, or haddock, filleted
juice of 3–4 lemons
3 onions, skinned and grated, then squeezed to extract the juice
10 ml (2 tsp) cumin seed, ground
2 garlic cloves, skinned and finely chopped
5 ml (1 tsp) paprika
Maldon or sea salt
freshly ground black pepper
about 45 ml (3 tbsp) olive oil
To serve
finely chopped parsley
lemon wedges
paprika (optional)

Cut the fish into chunks about 2.5 cm (1 inch) square, and put in a large shallow dish. Mix the lemon and onion juices, the cumin, garlic and paprika with a good pinch of salt and lots of black pepper, then pour over the fish. Leave for at least 1 hour, turning two or three times.

Thread the fish onto skewers, and brush all over with olive oil. Grill, ideally over charcoal, otherwise under a medium heat for 5–6 minutes until golden. Serve on a mound of chopped parsley, with lemon wedges, and an extra dusting of paprika if wished.

Karidesli Tavasi
Deep-Fried Prawns

The waters of the Bosphorous provide a rich source of wonderful shellfish. Try to buy large, uncooked prawns – otherwise omit the poaching.

———————◆———————

SERVES 6

700 g–1 kg (1½–2¼ lb) large uncooked prawns
75 g (3 oz) salt
1 large egg, beaten
Maldon or sea salt and freshly ground black pepper
plain flour
olive oil, for deep frying
To serve
lemon wedges
Tarator Sade or Consbareyah (page 16)

———————◆———————

Uncooked prawns will usually have been shelled, apart from the small tail piece. If you are buying unshelled ones, buy the larger quantity and shell them yourself: pull off the head, then the legs. This will leave the body shell which easily peels away. Leave the tail piece. Devein. Bring a large pan of water – about 1 litre (1¾ pints) – to the boil, throw in the salt, let it bubble again, then add the prawns and cook for about 4–6 minutes. Test when the tail shell starts turning bright red – you don't want them underdone as they are slushy, on the other hand overcooking will toughen them. Drain on absorbent kitchen paper.

Dip each prawn in the egg, then season lightly with salt and freshly ground black pepper, and coat with flour.

Bring a large pan of oil – a good 5 cm (2 inches) – to smoking point, then add a few prawns at a time and fry quickly until golden, about 2–3 minutes. Drain thoroughly and serve with lemon wedges and *Tarator Sade* (page 16), or *Consbareyah* (page 16).

Karidesli Kimyon
Cumin Spiced Prawns

An adaptation of a *pilav* with prawns, given to me by a Turkish friend.

———————◆———————

SERVES 4–6

700 g (1½ lb) prawns, unshelled weight
5-cm (2-inch) piece lemon zest
3–4 parsley sprigs
6 white peppercorns
few celery leaves
45 ml (3 tbsp) olive oil
Maldon or sea salt
1 large onion, skinned and finely chopped
3–4 garlic cloves, skinned and finely chopped
5 ml (1 tsp) cumin seeds, lightly crushed
pinch of granulated sugar
pinch of cayenne pepper
freshly ground black pepper
30 ml (2 tbsp) finely chopped parsley
juice of ½–1 lemon

———————◆———————

Shell the prawns, throwing the shells and heads into a large saucepan. Cover well with cold water, add the lemon zest, parsley sprigs, peppercorns and celery leaves. Bring to the boil and simmer for about 45 minutes. Strain, and measure out 225 ml (8 fl oz) of the stock and reserve it. (Keep the rest for making soup, unless of course you are cooking a *pilav*, in which case you'll need about 300 ml (1 pint) of liquid.)

Heat the oil in a large frying pan, add the prawns and sauté quickly, just to colour. Remove with a slotted spoon, and sprinkle generously with salt. Add the onion and garlic to the pan, cook gently for 10 minutes until the onion has softened. Scatter in the cumin seeds, a pinch each of sugar and cayenne pepper, and a good grinding of black pepper. Stir well, then pour in the reserved stock and add the prawns. Bring quickly to the boil, then simmer – on the lowest possible heat – for about 10 minutes until the liquid is considerably reduced.

Transfer to a serving plate, scatter over the parsley and lemon juice to taste. Allow to cool to room temperature before serving, and accompany with nice hot *Pittas* (page 98).

LAHAM

◆

Meat

Strips of tender meat in slices,
Dipped in oil of finest make,
Tempt anew the flagging palate,
And the appetite awake.[1]

Throughout the whole of this vast region, the word meat is nearly always synonymous with mutton. True, you may be asked 'sheep mutton or goat mutton'? Goat mutton may even be the better choice, but mutton it will be. Anything else and it will usually be specified – and it will usually be lamb, apart from a few pork dishes in Greece and Cyprus. Lamb, or kid, roasted whole, are of course the traditional festive dishes. In Greece, at Easter, when the new young spring lamb is anticipated weeks ahead with much excitement and preparation. Elsewhere, whenever there is cause to celebrate – although occasionally a young gazelle, locally caught, may form the centrepiece of a desert banquet. But for centuries, sheep and goats have happily munched and foraged on the lightly-grassed hillsides and barren mountain tops, leaving the fertile valleys free for cultivation of vegetables. Nowadays, with more land reclaimed with sophisticated irrigation schemes, beef and veal[2] are becoming popular but they will still be cooked according to recipes unchanged through the ages, and lamb certainly still dominates the kitchen.

Since much of this lamb is certainly of an age to be legitimately classed as mutton, but without the advantages of a luscious living, the Middle Eastern cuisine has evolved a number of ways to produce an enormous range of dishes beautifully tender in texture and incredibly varied in flavour.

The methods used to achieve the requisite tenderness are twofold – both very simple. First, the meat is cut into very small pieces, and then it is marinated, sometimes for as long as 24 hours. Let not such simplicity be scorned however. For in these two steps the experience of centuries has been absorbed, refined and polished to great heights.

There is a further refinement in the preparation of meat which must be mentioned, since it forms a large – and supremely delicious – part of the Arab table. The meat, once cut, is minced and then pounded to a fine pasty mixture before being formed into small rissoles or patties. Forget though the grey-brown mess of school dinners, the thin breadcrumb-laden slabs that masquerade as beefburgers in Western supermarkets. The meatballs that come out of the Arab kitchen are succulent and tender, sweetly spiced, often subtly sauced, and infinite in their variety.

Şiş Kebab
Grilled Meat on a Skewer

Şiş kebabs (pronounced shish) are the kebabs most familiar to us in the West. In fact we have adopted the word kebab to mean anything put on a skewer and grilled, particularly over a barbecue. Whereas, kebab in Turkish merely means 'cooked meat' and it is şiş that is the skewer. The style of cooking undoubtedly was born with the bands of nomadic tribes, constantly pushed westwards across the plateaus from Lake Baykal towards Turkey. Precious fighting time could not be lost to the indulgences of haute cuisine, yet fighting, and fleeing, was hungry work. So they merely slew whatever animals they came across – usually sheep, cut up the carcasses, impaling the meat on their swords, then cooked it over the camp fire. Through the years, such refinements as marinades, herbs, spices and even vegetables have been added but it is still undoubtedly agreed that for the best flavour the skewers should be grilled over a wood or charcoal fire. The essence of simplicity has not been lost.

Today, this is a dish found all over Greece and Turkey – the subtle differences lie in the marinade seasonings. The recipe below uses a Greek marinade, the two following variations are Turkish. Tomatoes, onions and green peppers can also be interspersed with the meat – turning the Şiş kebabs into another favourite, Şaşlik.

———— ◆ ————

SERVES 4–6
900 g (2 lb) lean lamb, either fillet or boned leg
For the marinade
150 ml (¼ pint) olive oil
30–45 (2–3 tbsp) lemon juice
1 large onion skinned (optional)
15 ml (1 tbsp) rigani or oregano
3 bay leaves, crumbled
5 ml (1 tsp) black peppercorns, crushed
Maldon or sea salt

———— ◆ ————

Cut the meat into small cubes, removing any fat or tough sinews. Mix the oil with the lemon juice in a large bowl, then grate the onion into the bowl if using – some Greeks do, some don't (I like it). Add the rigani, bay leaves and peppercorns then mix in the meat and stir well. Leave covered for at least two hours – in Persia they let it stand for 12 hours, which makes the meat meltingly tender.

To cook, drain the meat and thread onto skewers, then put under a hot grill (or over a hot charcoal or wood fire – make sure it's neither flaming nor smoking) for about 7–10 minutes, constantly turning and basting with the marinade. The meat will be done when it is brown and crusty on the outside but still just pink in the middle. Sprinkle with salt, extra lemon if you wish, then serve with Pitta bread (page 98), cucumber and tomato salads.

Şaşlik
Meat and Vegetables on a Skewer

Pronounced 'shashlick', this is a very popular dish in Turkey. It's more substantial than the plain şiş kebab but for the meze table you can make a miniature version by chopping the meat and vegetables into quite small pieces, using cherry tomatoes if possible, but nice firm ones. The only disadvantage, to my mind, to this dish is that the tomatoes cook quicker than the onions or peppers, which obviously will still be fairly crunchy. But it is delicious. One other point, onions quartered will be difficult to thread onto the skewers, so cut them into five by cutting each curved side off, leaving a square central core.

———— ◆ ————

SERVES 6–8
900 g (2 lb) lamb, cubed
marinade (either page 53 or 54)
4 small tomatoes, quartered
4 small onions, skinned and cut into five pieces each
1 large green pepper, seeded and cut into 16 pieces
175 g (6 oz) button mushrooms
salt and freshly ground black pepper
To serve
lemon wedges
onion slices

———— ◆ ————

Marinade the meat in whichever marinade you prefer – traditionally it would be an oil and lemon juice one. Then thread the meat onto skewers, alternating each piece with a vegetable, dispersing the vegetables as evenly as possible. You may have a few pieces of onion left over.

Baste with the marinade and cook under a hot grill for 7–10 minutes, then sprinkle with salt and freshly ground black pepper. Serve with lemon wedges, slices of raw onion and a cucumber and tomato salad.

Turkish Marinaded Kebabs – I

In Turkey, sweet cinnamon is preferred to the pungent rigani, and paprika is sometimes added as well. Lemon juice is optional while the onion is usually grated and then sieved – to just extract the juice.

SERVES 4–6
For the marinade
150 ml (¼ pint) olive oil
juice of 1 large onion
juice of 1 lemon (optional)
5–10 ml (1–2 tsp) ground cinnamon
5 ml (1 tsp) paprika (optional)
5 ml (1 tsp) black peppercorns, crushed
900 g (2 lb lamb)
To serve
Maldon or sea salt
lemon wedges
finely chopped parsley

Mix all the marinade ingredients, excepting the salt, with the meat in a large bowl and leave, covered, for 2–12 hours. Cook as for Şiş Kebab (page 53), then serve with a sprinkling of salt, lemon wedges to garnish, on a bed of finely chopped parsley.

Turkish Marinaded Kebabs – II

Although not traditional, I also like using this for firm white fish such as cod steaks or monkfish.

60 ml (4 tbsp) olive oil
300 ml (½ pint) natural yogurt
juice of 1 medium onion
5 ml (1 tsp) black peppercorns, crushed
5 ml (1 tsp) cumin seeds, crushed (optional)
10 ml (2 tsp) paprika (optional)
900 g (2 lb) lamb
Maldon or sea salt

Mix together the oil, yogurt, onion juice and black peppercorns. Add either the cumin seeds or paprika, then stir in the meat and leave for 2–12 hours. Cook in the usual way, sprinkle with salt before serving with *Pitta* (page 98) and a cucumber salad. Garnish the salad with chopped parsley or dried mint.

Mi'Laaq Mashwi bi Toum
Grilled Liver with Garlic

I never liked liver much as a child – until the summer we went to Beirut. Persuaded to try this dish (the smell of garlic was, once again, the appetite-whetter!) it became a daily ritual. Grilled, as here, it is usually served hot, but there is an equally good cold version, in which case the liver pieces are quickly fried in hot oil – for no more than 1 minute or so though, otherwise it becomes dry and leathery. Turkey also has her version of this, called çiger kebab (liver kebab) but the liver is merely salted and brushed with oil before cooking, then served with raw sliced onions, chopped parsley, tomatoes and lemon wedges. Kidneys are sometimes alternated with liver, or mushrooms particularly in Iraq.

SERVES 4–6
4–6 slices of liver, each about 1 cm (½ inch) thick
3–4 garlic cloves, skinned
Maldon or sea salt
60 ml (4 tbsp) olive oil
freshly ground black pepper
15 ml (1 tbsp) dried mint
juice of 1–2 lemons

Cut the liver into small pieces and put in a bowl. Crush the garlic with about 2.5 ml (½ tsp) of salt, then mix with the oil, lots of black pepper and the dried mint. Pour over the liver, stirring well, and leave, covered, for about 1 hour. (Purists say you should rub the crushed garlic into the liver pieces but I find this a bit too messy for my liking and I defy anyone to notice a difference in taste.)

Thread the meat onto skewers and grill under a medium heat for 3–4 minutes until nicely browned on the outside but still a bit pink inside. Baste after a couple of minutes with the marinade. Sprinkle with lemon juice and serve with almost anything you like except, say the Lebanese, yogurt which they believe to be incompatible with liver. It is almost the only time yogurt does not appear on the table.

Coriander'li
Coriander Sausages

In Cyprus the smell of sausages cooking is enhanced by the coriander seed flavouring, sweet and orangey. Sometimes chopped fresh coriander leaves are added, as is some finely chopped or crushed garlic. Saltpetre is available from chemists.

———— ◆ ————

Makes about 24 sausages

700 g (1½ lb) belly of pork, cut into strips, rinds removed
700 g (1½ lb) lean pork, preferably hand and spring
30 ml (2 tbsp) salt
freshly ground white pepper
22.5 ml (1½ tbsp) granulated sugar
1.25 ml (¼ tsp) saltpetre
30 ml (2 tbsp) coriander seed, finely ground
2 garlic cloves, skinned and chopped or crushed (optional)
30 ml (2 tbsp) finely chopped coriander leaves (optional)
sausage skins (optional)
lard, for frying

———— ◆ ————

Cut all the pork into chunks and then put through the fine blade of a mincer twice or whizz for a few minutes in a food processor until very finely chopped. Mix in a large bowl with the remaining ingredients, except the skins, making sure all the seasonings are well and evenly distributed. Either put into the skins – or get your friendly butcher to do it for you, twisting the skins every six inches or so, then hang in a dry, airy place for 1–2 days. This improves the flavour enormously but is not an essential, then dip into boiling water for one second before grilling or frying in a very little lard.

If you can't get – or cope with the sausage skins, leave the mixture overnight in the refrigerator, then form into sausage shapes or small patties and again, either grill or fry in a little lard. Cook them slowly for about 15–20 minutes longer than you would bought packaged sausages as the meat content is 100 per cent, as opposed to about 70 in even the best bought sausage.

Doner Kebab
The Revolving Kebab

All over Turkey there are small eating places, with just a few bare tables, and the huge vertical spit with an apparently enormous hunk of meat slowly, but endlessly, revolving around a three-sided charcoal fire. *Don* means to 'turn around', hence the name for what is now a familiar sight in the West, and a food that we take very much for granted. But it takes a great deal of expertise to prepare this outlandish sausage, and it is a technique I find fascinating although I have not yet been brave enough to try it. I was sorely tempted one day, after a demonstration in a small Turkish restaurant in London. Like all experts, they made it look so dreadfully simple but I'm afraid reality set in once back in my own kitchen. However, for those fearless cooks who wish to try it, an ordinary rôtisserie spit can be used (although the meat will take longer to cook), and I think it is interesting anyway to see how the Turks have evolved the *kebab* into this difficult but particularly delicious dish.

The meat from the hindquarters of the lamb (the loin and chump chops in English butchery) is cut into long, fine strips, all fat and tough sinews removed, then pounded until almost paper-thin and marinated for 24 hours in oil, milk, lemon and finely sliced onions. After draining, each slice is spread with warm lamb fat and then (this is the tricky bit) tightly wound round an enormous skewer, beginning at the middle, then up to each end, strip by strip building up that huge sausage, enormously fat in the centre and tapering off at each end, the whole being continually pressed, then trimmed at the finish to make a smooth and neat shape. The spit is fixed vertically in front of a three-sided, many-tiered charcoal brazier to begin its perpetual pirouette. As the meat on the outside becomes crusty and browned, it is carved off, to be eaten instantly with fresh mint or parsley, *raki* of course, while the rest continues its slow dance, while the next customers impatiently waiting. Until nothing is left.

In Syria, there is a dish similarly made with veal. Called *shawmirmah*, the meat is marinated in a huge range of spices, including fenugreek, cardamom, coriander, mastic and often a whole head – or two – of garlic.

Kofta

Minced Meat

Here, in *koftas*, minced meat rissoles or meatballs, grilled or fried, steamed or poached, have the Arabs displayed their greatest inventiveness in transforming the otherwise tough and inedible into a supreme delicacy. Despite the same basic recipe, the ways of preparing them are legion. Once, when I had tasted seven – very different – *koftas* in as many days, I asked 'How many *koftas* are there?' Our cook, who was a poetic soul and devoured Arabic poetry much as I devoured his food, replied 'They are as numerous as the stars in the firmament'. It became my favourite phrase for weeks thereafter.

I am still discovering new variations, and I have given a goodly number below, not only because I think they are delicious but they are simple to make, requiring only time (and even that is banished if you have a food processor), a decently stocked spice cupboard and a little imagination. Lamb is the meat usually used but all are equally good with beef, or a mixture of both. Veal is sometimes used in Syria, although it seems a little extravagant when it is so expensive in England but pork could well be substituted – though this would of course be forbidden in the Middle East. Of paramount importance to the tenderness and succulence of this dish, is the texture of the meat. You must pound it until absolutely pasty – in a food processor this takes a matter of minutes. Otherwise, put the meat through a mincer – even if you buy it already minced – at least once, if not twice, then bash it with a wooden spoon against the sides of a large bowl until you have a really pasty mass (I know this sounds rather horrid but it is descriptive, and you will be rewarded with the glorious smell of the spices, and the delicious end result). Keep your hands wetted with cold water while forming the rissoles, for the minimum of mess and the neatest of shapes. And if you flatten them into beefburgers, even the most timid of children (gastronomically, that is) will eat them – and ask for more. Keep the seasonings simple at first, then experiment to find those you like best.

SERVES 6

900 g (2 lb) lamb, beef or a mixture, minced and pounded
2 large onions, skinned and minced or grated
salt and freshly ground white or black pepper
5 ml (1 tsp) ground cinnamon (optional)
plus 5 ml (1 tsp) paprika (optional)
or 5 ml (1 tsp) cumin seeds, crushed (optional)
plus 5 ml (1 tsp) ground allspice or dried mint (optional)
or 5 ml (1 tsp) coriander seeds, ground (optional)
plus 30 ml (2 tbsp) finely chopped parsley (optional)
1–2 garlic cloves, skinned and crushed or finely chopped
To serve
Pittas *(page 98)*
chopped parsley
lemon wedges

———————♦———————

Mix everything together in a large bowl, having pounded the meat first. Or whizz the meat in a food processor, then add the onion and spices of your choice (white pepper will give a slightly spicier taste than black), and whizz again. Form the meat into small balls and thread on a skewer (the flat-edged type are best) or shape like a sausage round the skewers. Lightly oil the grill grid or barbecue grid to avoid the meat sticking, then cook under a high heat (non-smoking, glowing barbecue) for about 4–7 minutes until nicely browned and crispy on the outside but still tender and juicy within. Serve tucked into warm pittas, with chopped parsley, lemon wedges and a selection of salads.

Brochettes

In Morocco, the French influence is revealed in their name for *koftas* – *brochettes*. Miniature versions, laden onto tiny skewers, and spiced with a pinch of almost everything the spice cupboard has to offer, but so subtly there is just one glorious rich flavour – the component parts almost impossible to identify so well blended are they. *Felfa soudania* is a ground spice from exceedingly hot peppers, native to North Africa and Senegal – use *Harissa* (page 19) instead unless a kind friend (kind only if you happen to love hot chillies!) can bring some back from Morocco for you. *Ras el hanout* I found – once – in Paris, but never, so far, in England. It is an incredibly complex blend of spices, including cardamom, mace, nutmeg, several types of peppers – hot and sweet, ginger, cloves, cinnamon, ash-tree fruits, something I found translated as 'belladonna berries' – obviously *not* what we would mean by belladonna, and several other spices which I have, yet, not been able to equate with anything we know in the west. Do not attempt to make it, simply omit.

———— ♦ ————

SERVES 6–8

900 g (2 lb) lamb or beef, minced and pounded
75 g (3 oz) lamb or beef fat, chilled then minced
1 large onion, skinned and grated
1 small bunch parsley, finely chopped
1 small bunch fresh coriander leaves, finely chopped
10 ml (2 tsp) paprika
5 ml (1 tsp) cumin seeds, ground
good 5 ml (1 heaped tsp) ground cinnamon
pinch of felfia soudania or 1.5–2.5 ml (¼–½ tsp)
    Harissa *(page 19)*
2.5 ml (½ tsp) ras el hanout
Maldon or sea salt
4–5 sprigs fresh mint, very finely chopped

———— ♦ ————

Mix the pounded meat with the minced fat, blending evenly (the fat melts during the cooking, making these extraordinarily succulent). Then mix together the grated onion with all the herbs and spices – this helps to distribute them all through the meat – and add to the meat, stirring quite thoroughly. Season fairly generously with salt. Then take a lump of meat, about the size of a small egg, and shape into a thin sausage on a skewer – or into long thin fingers, if you haven't skewers. Lightly oil a grill grid and cook under a high heat for 3–5 minutes until browned on the outside. Traditionally served with mint tea.

Kufta Isbanish Kharouf
Spinach and Lamb Meatballs

Spinach, or chard, is a much loved vegetable in Iraq, Persia and Syria. I have also used fresh beetroot tops very successfully as a substitute, but fresh is the word.

———— ♦ ————

SERVES 4–6

700 g (1½ lb) fresh spinach
700 g (1½ lb) lamb, minced and pounded
2 slices of white bread, crusts removed
2 eggs, beaten
salt and freshly ground white pepper
1.5 ml (¼ tsp) ground fenugreek
5 ml (1 tsp) ground allspice
60 ml (4 tbsp) olive oil
juice of 1 large lemon
juice of 2 limes

———— ♦ ————

Wash and trim the spinach, then cook until softened in a large pan with 30 ml (2 tbsp) of water to prevent sticking. Drain, chop and mix with the meat. Soak the bread in cold water for 5 minutes, then squeeze dry and crumble and pound well into the meat mixture. Beat in the eggs and seasonings until pasty, then form into small balls or, as our cook used to do, long small fingers.

Heat 45 ml (3 tbsp) of the oil in a frying pan, add the meatballs and cook for 3–4 minutes until browned all over. Drain the pan of the used oil, add the remaining fresh oil, the lemon and lime juice and enough water to not quite cover the meatballs, about 100–150 ml (4–5 fl oz). Bring quickly to the boil, then simmer very gently, covered, for about 10 minutes, until the liquid is absorbed and the meat is tender.

Khoreshe Mast

Meatballs with Yogurt

From Persia come these subtly spiced meatballs, in a creamy yogurt sauce delicately tinged with saffron.

◆

SERVES 6

800 g (1¾ lb) lamb, minced and pounded
2 large onions, skinned
salt and freshly ground black pepper
5 ml (1 tsp) dried dill
large pinch of ground fenugreek
45 ml (3 tbsp) olive oil
10 ml (2 tsp) cumin seeds
10 ml (2 tsp) coriander seeds
6 whole cloves
5-cm (2-inch) piece cinnamon bark
8 cardamom pods
3 saffron strands
juice of 1 lime
175 ml (6 fl oz) natural yogurt
2.5 ml (½ tsp) cornflour

◆

Put the meat into a large bowl, then add one of the onions, either grated or minced. Season fairly highly with salt and freshly ground black pepper, add the dill and fenugreek and mix thoroughly. Form into small meatballs and keep aside. Heat the olive oil in a frying pan, meanwhile grind the spices – having taken the cardamom seeds out of their pods – then add to the pan and cook for about 1 minute until they start to smell aromatic. Slice the remaining onion finely and add to the pan. Let it fry for 6–7 minutes until softened.

Crumble the saffron strands into a measuring jug, then pour on 175 ml (6 fl oz) of boiling water and let it stand for 5 minutes. When the onions are soft, add the meatballs to the pan – push the onions to the sides – and cook, constantly turning until browned all over, about 4–5 minutes. Pour on the saffron water (and the strands), and the lime juice, mix together, then simmer gently for about 20–25 minutes until the water has been almost absorbed.

While the meatballs are cooking, stabilise the yogurt by first whisking in a pan until smooth and 'thin', then mix the cornflour with a little cold water. Stir into the yogurt with a good pinch of salt, and constantly stirring with a wooden spoon in the same direction (this is vital), bring gently to the boil. Leave to simmer, *uncovered*, for about 10 minutes until it is fairly thick. Then remove from the heat – it is now ready to be used and can be cooked, even boiled, for as long as necessary, without curdling. The yogurt we had in the Middle East was made from salted goat's milk, as it has been from time immemorial, and so never curdled. But home made, or bought, yogurt which is made from cow's milk will, unless stabilised. It makes no difference to the taste of the dish but it does slightly mar the appearance.

When there is a scant 15 ml (1 tbsp) of liquid left in the pan, stir in the yogurt and cook, gently, for another 5–15 minutes depending on how much sauce you want left with the meatballs. I like a little, very thick, sauce, especially if serving cold. Others prefer to have more sauce particularly when serving hot, with rice.

Kufteh Mo'alla

Stuffed Meatballs

Another superb variation from Persia – an extremely sophisticated version of Scotch eggs. A few tablespoons of tomato purée are sometimes added to the broth in other countries, with the prunes, split peas and pistachios omitted. In Persia, mint tea is often used to soak the prunes, and if the dish is to be served as a main course, the quantity of broth would be doubled, giving a small bowl of soup as a starter.

◆

SERVES 4–8

75 g (3 oz) yellow split peas, soaked overnight
900 g (2 lb) lamb, minced and pounded
1 onion, skinned and minced or grated
45 ml (3 tbsp) finely chopped dill
about 25 g (1 oz) pistachios (unshelled weight)
8 prunes, stoned and soaked for 2 hours in cold
  water or tea
Maldon or sea salt
freshly ground black pepper
5 ml (1 tsp) ground cinnamon
4 eggs, hard-boiled and shelled
2–3 strands saffron
450 ml (¾ pint) light stock, preferably veal
about 45–60 ml (3–4 tbsp) flour
60–75 ml (4–5 tbsp) olive oil
juice of 1 large lemon
pinch of granulated sugar
15 ml (1 tbsp) finely chopped fresh mint
15 ml (1 tbsp) finely chopped fresh basil

◆

Rinse the split peas, put in a pan with water to cover by a good 5 cm (2 inches) and bring to the boil, then gently simmer until the peas are quite soft but not mushy. This will take about 30 minutes to 1 hour, depending on the age and freshness of the peas. Drain and mix with the meat, onion, dill, a generous seasoning of salt and pepper and the cinnamon.

Shell the pistachios, drain the prunes and stuff each with 3–4 nuts. Divide the meat into four, rolling each piece into a large ball, then push your thumb through to the centre and make a good cavity in the middle. Insert a prune, then an egg, then another prune, and close up again, making sure the join is well sealed.

Bring the stock to the boil, pour over the saffron strands and leave for 5 minutes. Lightly flour the meatballs, heat the oil in a large shallow pan until nearly smoking, and cook the balls, turning gently but constantly until they are golden all over. Drain off any oil in the pan, then pour in the stock and saffron, the lemon juice and add a pinch of sugar. Bring slowly to the boil, then simmer for about 25–30 minutes, until the meatballs are thoroughly cooked and the sauce is much reduced. Either serve hot, sprinkled with the mint and basil, or transfer into a dish, pour over the sauce and the herbs and cool, before cutting into slices.

Kadin Budu

Ladies' Thighs

The Turks have the most picturesque names for their dishes – Ladies' Navels, Girl's Fingers, Liar *Dolmas*. These soft, juicy meatballs with their crispy outer shells are first simmered in a little water to trap the juices, then quickly fried in hot fat. There is another similar dish, *summakli köfte* (meatballs with *sumac* – with the added spice for some reason they cease to be ladies' thighs!) which substitutes grated potato for the rice, and serves them on toasted bread, covered in yogurt with a little *sumac* sprinkled over. The Greek *Keftedhes* substitute breadcrumbs for rice and their favourite *rigani* for the other spices. All are good.

SERVES 4–6

700 g (1½ lb) lamb, minced and pounded
50 g (2 oz) rice
1 or 2 large eggs
5–15 ml (1–3 tsp) olive oil (optional)
1 medium onion, skinned and grated or minced
15 ml (1 tbsp) coriander seeds, lightly ground
2–3 garlic cloves, skinned and crushed
salt and freshly ground black pepper
5 ml (1 tsp) dried mint
or finely chopped fresh parsley
5 ml (1 tsp) finely chopped fresh dill (optional)
oil or unsalted butter, for frying
plain flour (optional)
To serve
lemon wedges

Mix the meat with the rice. Then either whisk one egg until frothy, with or without 5 ml (1 tsp) olive oil – this is purely a matter of personal taste, then mix well into the meat. Or, add 15 ml (1 tbsp) of oil to the meat, and no egg. Recipes vary greatly on this point – I have even seen some without egg or oil, but I think one or the other adds to the succulence of the meatballs. Add the onion, spices and herbs of your choice, again mixing thoroughly, then leave the mixture to stand for 1 hour, to let the flavours permeate.

Form the meat into small balls, wetting your hands as necessary, then arrange in one layer in a large shallow pan. Put just enough water to cover the bottom of the pan, about 1 cm (½ inch), 150–175 ml (5–6 fl oz), cover and cook gently for 15–20 minutes until the water has all been absorbed and the meat looks cooked. Remove from the pan and cool.

Beat the other egg, again until frothy, and dip the meatballs quickly into it. Heat enough oil or butter to cover the surface of the pan, about 30–45 ml (2–3 tbsp) and when hot, quickly dip the meatballs in flour if you wish (I don't, but many cooks like the extra crispness it gives) and put into the pan. Cook for a few minutes until browned and crisp all over, then serve with lemon wedges, rice, *Pittas* (page 98), and salads.

Kabak ve Köfte
Courgette and Lamb Meatballs

From Izmir, on the Aegean coast of Turkey, comes this unusual combination. It was not far from here, near Ephesus (Efes, in modern day Turkey) that the Virgin Mary settled after Christ died, to spend a peaceful old age. A simple chapel stands as a shrine on the site of her house, while a few miles away are the ruins of the ancient Greco-Roman town which, in her day, must have been magnificent with, no doubt, a thriving market place.

Aubergines are sometimes substituted for the courgettes as both grow prolifically in the area. If you use aubergines don't peel or grate them, just cut into chunks before salting them. You may need a little extra oil for the cooking.

------------♦------------

SERVES 6–8

700 g (1½ lb) courgettes, peeled
salt
30–45 ml (2–3 tbsp) olive oil
2 medium onions, skinned and finely chopped
1–2 garlic cloves, skinned and crushed
700 g (1½ lb) lamb, minced and pounded
75 g (3 oz) Feta cheese, grated
15 ml (1 tbsp) dried mint
2 eggs
freshly ground black pepper
plain flour
vegetable oil, for frying

------------♦------------

Cut the courgettes in half, lengthways, sprinkle with salt and leave for 1 hour. Rinse thoroughly, squeeze, then grate them. Heat the oil in a large frying pan, add the onions and gently sauté until softened, about 5 minutes. Add the garlic and the grated courgette, and cook, gently, for 10–25 minutes, until tender. Remove from the heat and cool, then mix with the meat, cheese, mint and eggs. Season with salt and freshly ground black pepper, then pound until pasty.

Form into little balls, and roll quickly in flour. Heat a little oil, enough to cover the surface of the frying pan, until nearly smoking, then, on a very low heat, cook the meatballs for 10–15 minutes, turning them frequently until golden on the outside and cooked through. Very good hot, even better cold.

Daond Pasha
Meatballs with Pine Nuts and Tomatoes

Pine nuts, with their sweet, delicate flavour, are much loved, and much used in Syria. Meatballs stuffed with these nuts were a firm family favourite when we were in Damascus, where they were cooked, unusually, in the northern Syrian fashion – in the oven. When we moved to Kirkuk, in the north of Iraq, their sudden absence from the menu was loudly – and somewhat unreasonably – lamented by me. For Kirkuk, although spectacular in its 'burning fiery furnace'[1] into which King Nebuchadnezzar threw Meshach, Shadrach and Abednego, had little to offer in the way of food, except, surprisingly enough, tomatoes. Our cook made wonderful sauces from these, particularly for meatballs, which I had to concede were very good, but . . . Then, the blissful day arrived. Visitors from Aleppo, bearing gifts – of pine nuts. I later discovered that this marriage of pine nuts, tomato sauce and meatballs was a traditional dish of the Lebanon as well as Egypt, although tomato purée is used rather than whole tomatoes. For me, however, the dish will forever be Kirkuk.

------------♦------------

SERVES 6

75 ml (5 tbsp) olive oil
100 g (4 oz) pine nuts
900 g (2 lb) lamb or beef, minced and pounded
1 large onion, skinned and grated or minced
60 ml (4 tbsp) finely chopped parsley
5 ml (1 tsp) ground allspice
2.5 ml (½ tsp) ground ginger
Maldon or sea salt
freshly ground white pepper
1 large beef steak tomato, or 225 g (8 oz) plum
*   tomatoes, or 60–75 ml (4–5 tbsp) tomato purée*
pinch of granulated sugar
juice of 1 lemon

------------♦------------

Heat 30 ml (2 tbsp) of the oil in a frying pan, add the pine nuts and sauté gently for 2–3 minutes until they turn golden-pink. Drain. Mix the meat with onion, parsley, allspice, ginger, a good pinch or two of salt, and freshly ground white pepper, until quite pasty. Form into balls a bit smaller than a small egg, then push your finger through to the centre of each one, moving it around a little in the middle to make a pocket. Pour a scant 5 ml (1 small tsp) of nuts into each cavity, then firmly close the meat up again. (If you wish, you can reserve some pine nuts so that each meatball can be garnished with one stuck into the top, after cooking).

Heat the remaining oil, until nearly smoking, then cook the meatballs for 4–5 minutes until browned all over. While they are cooking, blanch the tomato or tomatoes (if you can get fresh plum tomatoes – or use canned ones, and weigh them after draining), then blend to a purée with about 30 ml (2 tbsp) of water. When the meatballs are cooked, add the tomato purée to the pan, with a pinch of sugar and half the lemon juice. Add a little more water to the pan if necessary to come just about level with the meatballs, then season lightly and simmer gently for about 15–20 minutes until the sauce has been absorbed. Add another spoonful of water or so, if the sauce evaporates too quickly. Sprinkle over the extra lemon juice, and a bit more chopped parsley if you wish. Traditionally served hot with rice, but also very good cold.

Choua

Steamed mutton

Steamed mutton, or lamb, is an unusual and delicate speciality of Morocco. Simply flavoured with salt and cumin seeds, the lamb is beautifully tender and juicy.

———— ◆ ————

SERVES 4–6
900 g (2 lb) boned leg of lamb
Maldon or sea salt
15 ml (1 tbsp) cumin seeds, lightly crushed

———— ◆ ————

Cut the meat into small cubes, trimming off all fat and sinews. Bring plenty of water to the boil in the bottom part of a steamer, put the lamb in the top, cover tightly and steam gently for 1¾–2 hours. If you don't have a steamer with a hermetic seal, stretch a clean tea towel over the top of the steamer and then fix the lid on firmly (tie the ends of the towel over the pan lid so they don't burn on the cooker). When the meat can be pulled apart with the fingers, it is done. Pile onto a serving platter, sprinkle lightly with salt and about 5 ml (1 tsp) cumin. Serve with rice, or *Pittas* (page 98) and salads, with a bowl of salt and the remaining cumin in a little bowl so that people can help themselves to extra if they wish.

Mukh Muhmmar

Fried Brains

In Turkey and Iraq particularly fried brains are popular. I find this a good way, too, to introduce people to brains – many are prejudiced against them due to the very softness of their texture. Here, the crispy crunchy outside forms an ideal contrast.

———— ◆ ————

SERVES 4
4 sets lamb's brains or 2 sets calf's
15 ml (1 tbsp) vinegar
salt
juice of ½ a small lemon
about 45 ml (3 tbsp) plain flour
1 egg
freshly ground white pepper
5 ml (1 tsp) ground allspice
5 ml (1 tsp) paprika (optional)
75–90 ml (5–6 tbsp) homemade, dried finely
    ground breadcrumbs
olive oil, for frying
To serve
chopped parsley
lemon or lime wedges

———— ◆ ————

Soak the brains in cold water, into which you have stirred the vinegar, for 1 hour. Rinse under a cold tap and carefully take off the thin membranes, then put into a pan, cover with boiling water, add a good pinch of salt and the juice of ½ a small lemon. Simmer for 3–4 minutes until beginning to firm up, then remove and dry on absorbent kitchen paper.

Sprinkle the flour on a shallow plate, beat the egg with freshly ground white pepper, the allspice and paprika if using, and spread the breadcrumbs on another plate. Cut the brains into small pieces, roll each one in the flour, dip into the egg, then roll in the breadcrumbs, making sure they are well coated. Heat a good 5 cm (2 inches) of olive oil in a deep pan until nearly smoking, then cook a few pieces at a time for about 4 minutes until they are nicely golden all over. Drain thoroughly and serve generously sprinkled with chopped parsley and lemon wedges or, even nicer, as we had in Iraq with lime wedges. Good hot or cold.

Kibbeh

Minced Meat with Burghul

The national dish of Syria and the Lebanon in whatever form, and it has many. Raw (the Arab answer to steak tartare) is one of the most popular, although in Syria *tray kibbeh* is almost equally loved. Then so are the long 'fingers' of *kibbeh* stuffed with a few pine nuts – Syrian women are said to be endowed by the gods if they have a long finger favoured for the making of these rissoles. And to watch them at work is fascinating. First, the pounding – even more dramatic than normal. I can remember hearing the hammering – which invariably began as poor Mademoiselle Dupont was vainly trying to instil the three 'R's into her class of small multi-nationals who gathered in our flat in Damascus each morning. The instant it began, our attention was lost. For, when silence fell, we knew we would be allowed to go and watch the cook's young and very beautiful wife making the *kibbeh*. With a swift, deft movement a handful of that pasty mixture would be whipped around her middle finger, caressed into an elongated smoothness, then slipped off, ready to be filled with the exquisitely sweet nuts. Ten minutes later, row upon row of slim, perfectly shaped and even sized 'shells' were lying on the long brass tray. She would present it to her husband, give a small bow to us wide-eyed children and the Mam'selle and quietly disappear into the nether regions. Her husband, of course, greatly enjoyed the reflected glory that it gave him, and he would stand, arms folded across his chest, smiling indulgently while she made them, nodding enthusiastically as the tray was filled. For this also betokened a happy occasion, *kibbeh* never being served at times of sadness, like a funeral or when a member of the family was going away – both events frequent, alas.

Kibbeh Nayye

Raw Kibbeh

♦

SERVES 6–8
125 g (4 oz) burghul (cracked wheat)
450 g (1lb) lamb, minced and well pounded
1 large onion, skinned and grated
Maldon or sea salt
freshly ground black pepper
freshly grated nutmeg
freshly ground allspice
cayenne pepper
cos lettuce, washed and drained
finely sliced onion rings
olive oil

♦

Put the burghul in a bowl, cover with cold water and leave to soak for about 10 minutes, then squeeze thoroughly to dry. Mix the burghul with the meat, grated onion, and the seasonings. The quantity here is very much a matter of taste. Traditionally it is fairly highly spiced, which I like, but it is advisable to begin with a little, adding a pinch of this, and a pinch of that, until you find it is right for you – this is half the fun of making *kibbeh* anyway! Pound, or whizz in a food processor until the mixture is really pasty – on a very hot day, I find it helps to add 15 ml (1 tbsp) or so of iced water. Then divide into 6 or 8 portions and pat into a neat, round shape, slightly domed in the middle.

Make a fan of cos lettuce leaves on individual plates, put a portion of meat into the middle of each, then make an indentation in the domes with your thumb. Stew the onion rings around the meat, and pour a dribble of olive oil into each hollow just before serving.

Kibbeh bi Sanieh
Tray Kibbeh

A mixture similar to that used for *kibbeh nayye*, but with double the amount of burghul, is often formed into small cakes, or shaped round skewers, and then either fried or grilled to be served crispy and hot. Even more delicious, and ideal for the *meze* table since it is equally good hot or cold, is the popular Syrian *tray kibbeh* – the basic mixture sandwiching cooked lamb, onions and pine nuts.

———————◆———————

SERVES 8–10

225 g (8 oz) burghul (cracked wheat)
450 g (1 lb) lamb, minced and well pounded
1 large onion, skinned and grated
Maldon or sea salt
freshly ground black pepper
freshly grated nutmeg
freshly ground allspice
cayenne pepper
For the stuffing
1 small onion, skinned and finely chopped
15 ml (1 tbsp) olive oil
225 g (8 oz) lamb or veal, minced
75 g (3 oz) pine nuts
salt and freshly ground black pepper
2.5 ml (½ tsp) ground cinnamon
5 ml (1 tsp) dried mint (optional)
100 g (4 oz) unsalted butter, melted
60 ml (4 tbsp) lamb or veal stock

———————◆———————

Soak the burghul in cold water for 10 minutes, then squeeze dry. Mix with the meat, grated onion, and seasonings to taste, pounding thoroughly until quite pasty.

To make the stuffing: sauté the onion in the oil until soft, spread the meat on top and stew gently for about 10–15 minutes, until lightly browned, adding the pine nuts, salt and freshly ground black pepper, cinnamon and mint after 5 minutes.

Brush a baking tin with a little of the melted butter, spread half the raw *kibbeh* mixture over the bottom, cover with the cooked meat, onions and pine nuts, then put the remaining *kibbeh* over the top. Run a knife round the edge of the tin, then cut the pie into lozenge shapes, small or large according to how you want to serve it. Sprinkle on the rest of the butter, and bake for 45 minutes to 1 hour in the oven at 190°C (375°F) mark 4, dribbling over 15 ml (1 tbsp) of stock every 10 minutes, until golden and crispy. Serve hot or cold with a large bowl of chilled yogurt.

Kibbeh Mahshi
Stuffed Kibbeh

These are the ultimate in *kibbeh* – long, thin, crispy shells filled with sweet, sweet pine nuts or, even more difficult to stuff perfectly, with a juicy meat filling. I must confess such is my addiction to pine nuts, that I always use them for a filling, but you can, if you wish – and are adept – use the stuffing for *Kibbeh bi Sanieh* (left). Wet your hands thoroughly both to make the shells and to stuff them, patching up any cracks with your thumb – again constantly dipped in cold water.

———————◆———————

SERVES 5–6

225 g (8 oz) burghul (cracked wheat)
450 g (1 lb) lamb, minced and well pounded
1 large onion, skinned and grated
Maldon or sea salt
freshly ground black pepper
freshly grated nutmeg
about 5 ml (1 tsp) ground cinnamon
50–75 g (2–3 oz) pine nuts
olive oil, for frying

———————◆———————

Soak the burghul in cold water for 10 minutes, then squeeze out, and mix with the meat, onion and seasonings. Pound until thoroughly pasty, then – with both hands wet – take a small lump of meat, a little less than a medium-sized egg, and shape it around your middle or forefinger to an even thickness all over, wetting the shell if necessary to close up any cracks. Drop about 5 ml (1 tsp) of pine nuts into each shell, closing up the ends in a smooth oval shape.

Heat a good 5 cm (2 inches) of oil in a deep pan until nearly smoking, then carefully roll in two or three shells and fry for about 5 minutes, until browned and crispy all over. Do the cooking in small batches, until you get deft at it – if there are too many in the pan, they can stick together and then crack. Drain thoroughly and serve hot or cold with yogurt, tahina salad and vegetable salads.

DAJAJ
Chicken and Poultry

Next a chicken, full and tender,
Fattened many moons agone
And a partridge, with a fledgling,
Roast with care, and nicely done.[1]

Not a little poetic licence went into those lines, I feel, unless the chicken of a thousand years ago had a vastly different life style from today's. Reading through the hundreds of different stuffings, exquisite spicings, and careful cooking methods recommended by the medieval chefs, I suspect that the creature was as scraggy as the ones we knew. Nonetheless, a cause for celebration has to be heralded with a feast, and chicken is usually the chosen bird. So, the Arab imagination once again comes into play and chicken is lusciously married to all the exotic seasonings of the area. Scented and sweetened with rose-flower water, oranges, mulberries or plums; spiced with cinnamon, ginger, turmeric, cardamoms; sharply enhanced by vinegar, lemons, pomegranates; softened with yogurt, garlic and oil; made fruity with quinces, apples and rhubarb; nutty with pistachios, hazels, almonds, poppy seeds, pine or walnuts; earthy with chick peas and onions; freshly green with parsley, coriander, mint, marjoram, and savory – you could eat a chicken dish 'for eighteen moons' without a repetition of recipe. That repetoire exhausted, there is still the rest of the feathered world to choose from. Wild duck from the Caspian Sea and the Iraqi marshes; partridge, loved by the Greeks, Cypriots and Moroccans; pigeons, a favourite everywhere; woodcock, quail, snipe, sandgrouse. The poet spoke truly of the 'partridge, with a fledgling', for even the tiniest birds are viewed in relation to the kitchen, many of which our softer, Western hearts would regard as sacrosanct. Particularly, I suspect, the minute *beccaficio* (*becfigue*, *beccafichi*, *beccafico*, or *beccaficca* in kitchen Arabic). This little creature, the figpecker to us, is so tiny that in Cyprus it is pickled whole, even the bones softening in the vinegar made from their sweet fine wine, Commanderia. Each bird only provides one mouthful of that favoured delicacy. Trapped as he sits fattening himself on grape juice, or his favourite fruit the fig – sucking out flesh and seeds, this little bird was popular with our ancestors, known as the *oiselet de Chypre* in the Middle Ages. The Lebanese still cook them as we did, threaded on skewers and spit-roasted, often wrapped in vine leaves to heighten their fruity flavour.

Dajaj Mashwi bil Zait wa Tom

Grilled Chicken with Garlic

Popular everywhere, this simple but garlicky marinade totally transforms even the most boring of English chickens – or scrawny Arab ones. In the Lebanon, we had a favourite restaurant which served divinely tender baby poussin (highly nurtured by the owner, I suspect), and I often use these now for a dinner à deux. For the meze table, though, I make miniature kebabs, using the skinned breasts only, but you could equally well use a jointed chicken, or just the legs. Turn this into a Turkish dish by adding the juice of an onion, a little ground cinnamon and freshly ground black pepper.

———————◆———————

SERVES 6

6 chicken breasts, skinned and boned
4–6 garlic cloves, skinned
Maldon or sea salt
juice of 1–1½ lemons
90–120 ml (6–8 tbsp) olive oil
finely chopped parsley

———————◆———————

Cut the breasts into bite-sized cubes and put in a shallow dish. Crush the garlic with salt until quite pulpy.

Mix in the lemon juice, then whisk into the oil. Pour over the chicken, turning everything over, and leave, covered, for 1–4 hours, turning the pieces once or twice during that time.

Put a large amount of chopped parsley on a plate. Thread the chicken onto small skewers – I use small bamboo ones soaked in lemon juice (soaking stops them burning when grilling, the lemon juice gives a wonderful tang to the middle of each piece of chicken; but water will do just as well). Roll each skewer in parsley then cook under a hot grill – better still over a hot barbecue, oil the grid first – for about 4–6 minutes, turning them to golden all over, and basting with the marinade, or extra oil if necessary. Wonderful.

Dajaj Mashwi bil Tom wa Laban

Grilled Chicken with Garlic and Yogurt

On our second trip to Beirut, I had these – and immediately, and utterly disloyally, preferred them to all else. The yogurt does not flavour the chicken so much as tenderise it and make it succulent and juicy. In Egypt, they were prepared with cardamom pods and yogurt – also very good. And in Greece, a pot of yogurt is often poured over grilled chicken, simply marinaded in oil, lemon and garlic – with maybe a touch of marjoram or rigani added. I tend to use the leftover legs from the chickens whose breasts have already contributed to other dishes (the wings kept for later) but you can use breasts, or chicken pieces if you prefer.

———————◆———————

SERVES 6

6 chicken legs
2–3 garlic cloves, skinned
Maldon or sea salt
5 ml (1 tsp) paprika
5 ml (1 tsp) cinnamon
1.5–2.5 ml (¼–½ tsp) cayenne pepper
juice of 1 lemon
90–120 ml (6–8 tbsp) olive oil
90–120 ml (6–8 tbsp) natural yogurt
freshly ground black pepper
To serve
lemon wedges (optional)

———————◆———————

I don't usually skin the chicken legs but sometimes make the odd gash here and there in the deepest part of the flesh, particularly if they are very large. Crush the garlic with a little salt, then mix with the paprika, cinnamon and cayenne, to taste. Stir in the lemon juice, then add the oil and yogurt. Put the chicken legs into a deep dish and cover with the marinade. Turn several times to cover them completely, then leave for 3–5 hours – overnight in the refrigerator is even better. Add a little more yogurt or oil if necessary.

Sprinkle with salt and lots of freshly ground black pepper then cook under a high heat on the grill for about 20–40 minutes, turning constantly and brushing with the marinade until they are very crispy and deeply golden – I like them almost charred on the outside. Eat hot or cold, gorgeous, with lemon wedges.

Dajaj Mashwi bil Baharat
Grilled Chicken with Spices

Back home in Baghdad, our cook produced his own version of chicken *kebabs*, wonderfully spiced with cardamom, turmeric and allspice – a touch of the Moghuls filtering eastwards.

◆

SERVES 6

6 chicken breasts, skinned and boned
3 garlic cloves, skinned
Maldon or sea salt
8–10 cardamom pods, husks removed
5 ml (1 tsp) turmeric
freshly ground allspice
freshly ground white pepper
juice of 3 limes or 1–1½ lemons
90–120 ml (6–8 tbsp) olive oil

◆

Cut the meat into small pieces and put into a bowl. Crush the garlic well with some salt. Grind the cardamom seeds in a spice grinder, then mix with the turmeric, allspice and a good grinding of white pepper and whisk into the lemon juice. Add the garlic and oil and pour over the chicken. Leave for 2–4 hours, turning occasionally.

Thread onto small, soaked, skewers, as for, *Dajaj Mashwi bil Zait wa Tom* (page 65) and grill for 4–6 minutes until golden all over, basting occasionally.

Dajaj Ma' Khokh, Asl wa Lauz
Chicken with Prunes, Honey and Almonds

Visiting a Moroccan friend in London once, the day after she had given a huge family party, I sampled these. Traditionally served hot, they were absolutely wonderful cold, the sauce having set to a sweet-spicy glaze. Persia too cooks prunes, not to mention apricots and sultanas, with chicken, and there are several references to the combination in old cookery books but the countries in-between seem to have lost the habit – a pity, for it is very good.

SERVES 6–8

1 large chicken, weighing about 1.6 kg (3½ lb), jointed (see below)
Maldon or sea salt
freshly ground black pepper
5-cm (2-inch) piece of cinnamon bark
2 large onions, skinned and grated or minced
75–100 g (3–4 oz) unsalted butter
2–3 saffron strands
225 g (8 oz) prunes, soaked overnight
2.5 ml (½ tsp) ground ginger
2.5 ml (½ tsp) ground cinnamon
15 ml (1 tbsp) clear honey
30 ml (2 tbsp) peanut oil
75 g (3 oz) blanched almonds
30 ml (2 tbsp) sesame seeds

◆

Have the butcher joint the chicken into 6 or 8 pieces, and ask for the liver if possible. If you do get the liver, wash it and cut out any yellowish bits – one trace of them and the sauce will be quite bitter. I usually keep the wings back for other recipes but you can, of course, include them here. Rub the pieces all over with salt and lots of freshly ground black pepper (the recipe given to me states: '1 heaped soupspoonful pepper,' but I feel that it is a bit *too* much for most people's taste) then arrange them in a large heavy-based pan. Bury the cinnamon bark, and the liver if you have it, in the middle, then sprinkle over the onions. Cut the butter into small pieces and put on top, then bring about 350 ml (12 fl oz) of water to the boil and pour over the saffron. Stir to start its colour running, then pour over the chicken. Cover the pan, and cook over a moderate heat until you hear the liquid bubbling. Turn the heat down and simmer for 30–40 minutes until the chicken is quite tender. Turn it over several times during the cooking, adding boiling water if necessary. Remove chicken pieces and reserve.

Drain the prunes and add to the pan, together with the ginger and ground cinnamon (take out the cinnamon bark) and cook for 15 minutes. Then stir in the honey and boil the sauce hard until it is quite syrupy, about 4–7 minutes but this does vary. Check to see if it needs more salt and pepper (unlikely) then gently lay the chicken pieces on top of the sauce. Cover the pan and reheat chicken.

Heat the oil and quickly fry the almonds for 2–3 minutes until nicely golden, then drain well. Dry roast the sesame seeds or, wipe out the almond pan and fry them in that until coloured. Arrange the chicken on a large platter, pour over the sauce, then scatter almonds and sesame seeds on top. Excellent eaten immediately – even better the next day.

Dajaj Sofrito
Chicken Sofrito

Sofrito, a word of Spanish origin, is used to describe a method of cooking chicken, veal or fish, much loved in the southern-eastern band of Mediterranean countries. Like so many things, the end result belies the essential simplicity of this dish: poaching in oil, water, lemon and turmeric to give a chicken, softly touched with gold, sitting in its lightly jellied sauce of a pale primrose hue. A great favourite in Alexandria when I visited with my grandfather. And I have since met a Turkish variation, *Tavuk Jölesi*, which omits turmeric but actually makes aspic of the chicken stock. Pieces of the meat are then set between layers of the aspic mixed with parsley and slivered almonds – it is very pretty.

———◆———

SERVES 6–8
1 large chicken, weighing about 1.6–2 kg
  (3½–4½ lb)
juice of 1 lemon
30–45 ml (2–3 tbsp) olive oil
2.5 ml (½ tsp) turmeric
1 garlic clove, skinned and crushed
5-cm (2-inch) piece cinnamon bark
Maldon or sea salt
freshly ground white pepper

———◆———

Rinse the chicken inside and out and place in a large saucepan. Mix the remaining ingredients with about 300 ml (½ pint) of water and pour over the chicken. Bring to the boil quickly, then turn the heat to low and gently simmer, covered, for 50 minutes to 1¼ hours. This will depend on your chicken, and if you should be lucky enough to get a real boiling fowl, then of course it will be much longer. But in England they are hard to find, so I tend to use a free range roasting chicken. Turn the chicken quite frequently during the cooking time, and add a little more water if necessary, but don't swamp the animal. Once the chicken is quite tender, remove the pan from the heat and check the seasoning, adjusting if necessary, then leave until cool enough to handle.

Carve the chicken into nice chunky pieces and arrange on a platter – not too shallow, you want room for the sauce to set around the meat. If the sauce has started to jell you may need to warm it a little, then pour all over the chicken and let it get quite cold – overnight in a cold larder is fine. If chilling, then bring to room temperature before serving, unless it's blazing hot, in which case remove from the refrigerator about 10–15 minutes before serving. Excellent with all sorts of salads, and particularly good with any of the nut sauces.

Ajniha al Dajaj bil Limoun Hamidh wa Tom
Chicken Wings with Lime Juice and Garlic

This was a hot contender for 'favourite' whenever we went to Beirut. My only problem on those wonderful holidays was too much choice – and eyes considerably bigger than tum. I always buy chickens whole and then joint them at home – usually using the breasts for one dish, then the legs for another (sometimes even plainly roasted with a stuffing where the breasts would have been). The wings though are always instantly snipped off and added to my collection in the freezer. Then, when I have lots, we can have a huge plate of these.... You can now, conveniently, buy bags of frozen chicken wings in many supermarkets. Even better.

———◆———

SERVES 4–6
12 chicken wings
2–3 garlic cloves, skinned
Maldon or sea salt
juice of 3–4 limes, or 2 large lemons
pinch of cayenne pepper

———◆———

Wash the wings, and singe off any lingering feather ends. Crush the garlic well with about 1.5 ml (¼ tsp) salt until really pulpy, then rub a little on each chicken wing. Put into a bowl and squeeze over the lime or lemon juice. Leave for at least 1 hour, preferably 4–5, turning them occasionally so all parts get impregnated with the juice.

Put the wings into a pan, preferably sitting in one layer. Pour over the marinade and then just enough water to cover. Bring quickly to the boil, then lower the heat and simmer for 12–15 minutes, uncovered, until the chicken is done and most of the sauce reduced. Transfer to a serving dish, scraping up all the juices in the pan and pouring them over. Wonderful eaten immediately and, if there should be any leftover, they are almost better.

Ajniha al Dajaj Ma' Buzur Simsim

Grilled Chicken Wings with Sesame Seed

Returning home, once again our poor cook was inundated with tales of wonderful foods. I suppose it was not very diplomatic of me to keep regaling him with stories of all these glories I ate on holiday but he always seemed to rise to the occasion. The next day I was given a plate of these and, of course, he had regained my affections. I have not met them elsewhere in the Middle East so have tried to recreate them from memory. Even if time has played a few tricks I think they are very good.

SERVES 6

12 chicken wings
45 ml (3 tbsp) sesame seeds
1–2 garlic cloves, skinned and crushed
Maldon or sea salt
freshly ground white pepper
pinch of fenugreek
juice of 1 lemon
45–60 ml (3–4 tbsp) olive oil
To serve
finely chopped parsley

Wash the wings and singe off any feather ends. Dry fry the sesame seeds for 1–2 minutes until golden but not burnt, then tip into a bowl. Mix in the crushed garlic, salt, pepper, fenugreek and lemon juice. Then beat in the oil, little by little, until well emulsified. Pour all over the chicken wings and leave to marinate for 4–5 hours, turning occasionally. Grill under a high heat for 5–9 minutes, turning once, and basting with the marinade, until crispy and golden. Serve sprinkled with parsley. Heaven.

Çerkez Tavuğu

Circassian Chicken

Another very famous Turkish dish and one of the most splendid ways of serving chicken cold. It was, according to legend, named after the Circassian girls in the Sultan's harem – reputed to be among the most beautiful. Other countries of the Middle East have adopted this recipe with alacrity, simply using the nuts available in their locality. Walnuts are the Turkish choice, hazelnuts, almonds or even pine nuts are used elsewhere. I wouldn't recom-

mend mixing nuts, except pine nuts and almonds, because I personally feel the flavours become too jumbled, but many people do. Once again – the choice is yours.

SERVES 6–8

1 large chicken, weighing about 1.6–1.8 kg (3½–4 lb)
2 onions, skinned
2 cloves
2 leeks
few celery leaves
Maldon or sea salt
freshly ground black pepper
1 thick slice white bread, crusts removed
150 g (5 oz) walnuts
1–2 garlic cloves, skinned and crushed
15 ml (1 tbsp) walnut oil
paprika

Rinse the chicken, then put in a large pan with one onion quartered, one stuck with the cloves. Add the leeks, celery leaves, a pinch of salt and freshly ground black pepper and bring to the boil. Skim off any scum, then simmer gently, covered, for about 1 hour until the chicken is quite tender. Remove the chicken and strain the stock. Carve the chicken into large pieces, then put in a shallow dish covered with a little stock. Leave to cool, the stock will keep the cooling chicken juicy.

Soak the bread in a little stock for 5 minutes. Grind the walnuts until quite fine, then put in a pan with the bread, crumble it a bit, and add a scant 600 ml (1 pint) of the strained stock. Add the garlic and bring to the boil stirring constantly, and bashing the bread until it's completely pulverised. Cook until the sauce has thickened, almost to the consistency of a good mayonnaise – you can add a little more stock if necessary. Season with a little more salt and pepper.

Drain off the stock in which the chicken pieces are cooling, then arrange the chicken on a large serving platter. Completely cover with the sauce, then leave to cool, covered, and preferably not in the refrigerator because it kills the development of the flavours. Just before serving, mix the walnut oil with a little paprika and drizzle all over the top.

Koftit Ferakh
Fried Chicken Balls

Chicken is popular, too, minced and made into miniature *köfte*, seasoned variously with turmeric, ginger, fenugreek or sweet cinnamon and paprika. Nuts are often added to the mixture, pistachios in Iraq, pine nuts in Syria and the Lebanon. Driving from Damascus to Baghdad, we stopped quite late at a tiny roadside café – one table and four chairs outside the flat-roofed two-roomed dwelling – to 'stretch our legs and have a little something to eat'. By the time I had asked my innocent, and childishly logical question 'Why? Are they too short?' bowls of steaming hot chick peas topped with these crispy meatballs were being handed out through the glassless window (when the shutters were closed, so was the café). There was no choice – and we needed none. Sitting, singing 'Twinkle, twinkle little star' at the brilliant sparkles in that dark night and tucking into those succulent rissoles, I solemnly announced that I was the happiest person in the world! I think my parents would have been happier without the endless serenade – Damascus to Baghdad is quite a long drive – but it doesn't seem to have affected our penchant for this dish. It is still a family favourite.

––––––––– ◆ –––––––––

SERVES 4–6
3 chicken breasts, minced
2 slices white bread, crusts removed
50 g (2 oz) pine nuts
45 ml (3 tbsp) finely chopped parsley
1.5 ml (¼ tsp) turmeric
1 egg, beaten
Maldon or sea salt
freshly ground black pepper
plain flour
olive oil, for frying
juice of 1 lemon

––––––––– ◆ –––––––––

Put the chicken into a large bowl. Soak the bread in a little water for 5 minutes, then squeeze dry and crumble into the chicken. Add the pine nuts, parsley and turmeric and mix. Beat in the egg, then season with salt and pepper and mix very thoroughly until the mixture is quite soft and smooth. With wet hands, form into small balls – no bigger than a walnut, and I sometimes make them as small as a hazelnut, literally 'bite-sized'. Lightly sprinkle with flour, then heat a good 2.5 cm (1 inch) oil in a deep pan, and when nearly smoking, drop in a few balls. Cook for a few minutes until golden-

brown and crispy. Drain on absorbent kitchen paper and cook the rest the same way. Lovely hot, and cold, both sprinkled with lemon juice.

Koftit Ferakh
Chicken Balls

Another popular variation. Although cooked chicken can be used in the previous recipe, I prefer to use raw, it seems to be more succulent. But for this dish, already cooked chicken is a must if you don't want to fry the meatballs and I personally think they are best unfried, the crunchiness of the nuts contrasting pleasantly with the soft chicken.

––––––––– ◆ –––––––––

SERVES 4–6
350 g (12 oz) cooked chicken meat, off the bone
2 slices white bread, crusts removed
milk
75 g (3 oz) pistachios, shelled and very finely chopped
1.5 ml (¼ tsp) ground cinnamon
pinch of paprika
15–30 ml (1–2 tbsp) olive oil
juice of ½–1 lemon
Maldon or sea salt
freshly ground black or white pepper
finely chopped parsley

––––––––– ◆ –––––––––

Mince the chicken or put in a food processor and whizz until very finely chopped. Soak the bread in a little milk, then squeeze dry and crumble finely. Mix into the chicken, then add the pistachios, cinnamon and paprika. Stir in half the oil and lemon juice and season lightly. Knead until the mixture is thoroughly amalgamated, adding a little more oil or lemon if it's too thick, and according to taste. Adjust the seasoning if necessary, then roll thickly in the chopped parsley and chill slightly before serving.

Piliç Dolması
Stuffed Chicken

The first Turkish party I attended was quite an overwhelming affair, even by Middle Eastern standards. And in the middle of the table was a circle of eight golden, tantalising chickens. When our hostess came to carving them, she cut straight through. Aaha, I thought, boned chickens – impressive at the best of times. This was even better though, for the chicken flesh had been cooked, minced and mixed with veal and pistachios and then stuffed into the skin, for its final sautéeing. My first attempts to recreate this at home perforce had to omit the final stage since, by then, my chicken skin looked like a jigsaw puzzle, so I merely rolled the whole thing into a huge sausage and cooked that. It tasted excellent although it didn't look quite so awe inspiring. Then I learnt that that was the cheat's way. I still cheat, I'm afraid, whenever I can get to my friendly butcher. He does the whole job superbly, in about 1 minute flat. I am getting better, and I give his instructions – they sound so foolproof – below. With a word of warning, go slowly at first – whenever I try to ape his performance, the wretched skin catches on some protruding bone I didn't know existed, and rips.

––––––––◆––––––––

SERVES 8–12

1 large chicken, weighing about 1.8 kg (4 lb)
Maldon or sea salt
freshly ground black pepper
1–2 celery sticks
3–4 parsley sprigs
2 onions, skinned and quartered
450 g (1 lb) lean veal, minced
125 g (4 oz) pistachios, shelled
1 garlic clove, skinned and finely chopped
5 ml (1 tsp) ground cinnamon
juice of ½–1 lemon
75–90 ml (5–6 tbsp) finely chopped parsley
45 ml (3 tbsp) olive oil

––––––––◆––––––––

Rinse the chicken, then chop off the wings (keep for another recipe) and the tips of the drumsticks. Rub the chicken all over, quite roughly, to start loosening the skin from the flesh, and then, using a boning knife or one with a small thin blade, loosen the skin from the breast membrane by carefully running between the skin and the breasts. Be very gentle over the top of the breast bone as it can easily tear here, but if you have rubbed well, it should slide through easily enough. Now, sit the chicken on its 'tail' end and start pulling the skin down, from the neck, over the wing gaps, the body and finally the legs. It will be inside out when you have pulled it right off – and, hopefully, more or less in one piece. Wash, and turn the right way out.

The rest is easy. Put the chicken into a large pan, add a little salt and pepper, the celery, parsley and onions. Bring to the boil, skim, then simmer gently for about 1 hour until the chicken is beautifully tender. Let it cool in the stock until easily handled, then take out and cut off all the flesh. Strain the stock and reserve.

Mince the chicken, then mix with the veal, pistachios, garlic, cinnamon and juice of ½ lemon. Stir in the parsley and make sure everything is evenly distributed, then season, quite highly, with salt and pepper.

If you should be unfortunate enough to have any holes in your skin, darn them, and all other openings except the largest. Spoon the stuffing in, not too tightly – you don't want it to burst in the cooking after all this, then sew up the cavity. Mould it roughly into a chicken shape.

Heat the oil in a large pan, add the 'chicken' and fry on all sides until browned, about 4–5 minutes, then add a couple of ladles of the reserved stock and the remaining lemon juice. Cover the pan, and stew gently for about 1 hour, adding more stock by the ladle, when the last lot has almost disappeared. At the finish, you should have about two ladles of liquid, almost a glaze, left. Transfer to a serving dish. Leave to cool. To serve, cut into thick slices or show it off whole.

Hamaan Mechoui
Moroccan Grilled Pigeons

There was a restaurant near the Pyramids famous for its pigeons, which, alas, to me was only a legend. But again my grandfather 'told all' and a favourite supper of ours was fresh pigeon breasts, grilled according to his precise requirements, 'no, no, no, not enough lemon juice; a touch more pepper – more, and lots of chervil. Is it finely chopped? Good, that's good'. I must say I never once in my life saw him cook anything – but he always seemed to know how to cook everything, down to the last detail. Pigeons don't hold the same inhibitions for the English as the other birds favoured by the Middle East, so are widely available. But rarely fresh, except in the country where I find the neighbouring farmers are only too happy to slip you as many as you want virtually, and for the Egyptian dish, they are perfect. I was overjoyed then to be given a Moroccan recipe which gently stews the pigeons first, before grilling. The answer to my problems – and to the *meze* table. For the initial cooking can be done hours ahead, leaving only the final grilling before serving.

SERVES 4–6

4 pigeons, cleaned
50 g (2 oz) unsalted butter or 60 ml (4 tbsp) oil, if
  serving cold
10 ml (2 tsp) paprika
5 ml (1 tsp) cumin seeds, crushed
1 garlic clove, skinned and crushed
pinch of cinnamon
Maldon or sea salt
freshly ground black pepper

Wash the pigeons inside and out and put into a large pan, preferably sitting them snugly side by side tilted on one breast. Melt the butter if using, then mix with half the paprika and cumin seeds, the garlic, and cinnamon. Oil can just be stirred into the ingredients, then poured over the pigeons with about 600 ml (1 pint) of water. The pigeons should barely be covered. Bring to the boil, then cover the pan and simmer gently for 1½–2 hours until the birds are quite tender, adding a little more water if necessary, and turning the birds onto the other breast halfway through cooking. When they are done, remove from the pan and boil the sauce hard until it is much reduced – you'll need a scant 150 ml (¼ pint). Cool the sauce and the birds.

About 10 minutes before serving, stir the remaining paprika and cumin into the sauce. Cut the breasts off each bird (keep the remainder of the carcass for a glorious soup) and brush each breast, on both sides, with a little of the sauce. Sprinkle with salt and pepper and grill under a hot heat for 2–3 minutes on each side until crisping. Cut each breast into three slices on the diagonal, and serve hot or cold.

Partridges Klephti
Roasted 'Stolen' Partridges

Klephtis, from the Greek 'to steal' was a term originally applied to the Greek brigands who waged guerilla warfare against the occupying Turks. Soon it came to mean their method of cooking – meat, usually stolen, and particularly birds, stuffed with mountain herbs, wrapped in paper, then buried in an earthenware pot to cook over a glowing pinewood fire.

SERVES 4–6

2 young partridges, hung, then dressed
juice of 1 lemon
6 sprigs fresh thyme
6 sprigs fresh marjoram
Maldon or sea salt
freshly ground black pepper
4–6 rashers streaky bacon
butter or olive oil

Wash the birds inside and out then rub lemon juice all over them. Stuff the birds with 3 sprigs each of the herbs, then season with salt and black pepper and wrap in the bacon.

Liberally butter or brush with oil (I prefer the latter if the birds are going to be left to cool). Prepare 2 pieces of foil or baking paper large enough to completely envelop the birds. Put a bird in the centre of each paper, and seal firmly. Cook in the oven at 170°C (325°F) mark 3, for about 1–1½ hours – this will depend on the age and size of the birds. Check after 1 hour by piercing the breast – if the juices are clear, it's done. Or wiggle one of the legs, if it moves very easily, again it's ready. Take out of the oven, remove the bacon and discard the herbs, then joint into four pieces and serve with their juices poured over. If you want to serve them cold (I think very good) leave them to cool in their papers before jointing them. Excellent with cucumber and yogurt salad.

71

M'hammer Durraj
Fried Partridges

M'hammer is actually one of three basic sauces, which provide many subtle variations on a theme for the Moroccans. This is 'red' sauce, traditionally made with butter, paprika and cumin as the constants. Again, poussins can be substituted – and it's amazing what respectability this recipe gives to a frozen battery hen. If you can get fresh partridge – at the height of its season – then follow the Greeks and stuff the well larded bird with fresh herbs, bake in a very low oven *en papillote* for about 1–1½ hours.

SERVES 6
3 partridges, cleaned
2.5 ml (½ tsp) cumin seeds, crushed
2.5-cm (1-inch) piece fresh root ginger, peeled and grated
5 ml (1 tsp) paprika
5 ml (1 tsp) coriander seeds, ground
1 medium onion, skinned and minced or grated
1 garlic clove, skinned and crushed
Maldon or sea salt
freshly ground black pepper
100 g (4 oz) unsalted butter
60–75 ml (4–5 tbsp) peanut oil
2–3 strands saffron
bunch of coriander leaves
bunch of fresh parsley
¼ preserved lemon or 3 slices Limoun Hamadh Makbouss (page 82)

Wash the partridges inside and out and pat dry. Mix the spices with the onion and garlic, pounding until quite pulpy. Rub all over the partridges, smearing a little on the inside as well, then sprinkle some salt over them and lots of freshly ground black pepper. Melt half the butter and 15 ml (1 tbsp) of the peanut oil in a large pan or flameproof casserole dish, add the birds, breast side down and fry them for 3–4 minutes until golden all over. Pour 600 ml (1 pint) of boiling water over the saffron strands and stir until their colour starts to run, then pour over the partridges. Add a little more water if necessary, the partridges should be three-quarters covered, then tie the coriander and parsley together and tuck in the middle. Bring to the boil, then simmer, covered, for 30–45 minutes until the birds are tender. Older birds may need a little longer – do the leg pull test, if it moves easily, they're done. Take the birds out of the pan and cut each in half, using a cleaver or a good, heavy sharp knife.

Cut the peel away from the flesh of the lemon, then squeeze the flesh hard to extract as much juice as possible. Add to the sauce with the lemon zest, and boil hard to reduce to about 150 ml (¼ pint). If you want to make the dish to this stage in advance, don't reduce it quite so much, to allow for reduction on reheating.

About 15 minutes before serving, heat the remaining butter and oil. When very hot, add the partridge halves – you probably won't be able to do more than two at a time and fry until deeply golden. Drain and cook the rest. Reheat the sauce, discard the herb bunches, and pour over the partridges. Serve with lots of Arab bread, large napkins and bowls of rose-scented water. This is gutsy finger food.

Assafeer Meshwi
Grilled Quail

Sentiment, I'm afraid, does not rule the Mediterranean heart when it comes to the autumn flocks of migrating birds. From Italy and Greece to North Africa, the small birds are considered fair game, and many have their journey rudely ended in the cooking pot. These small birds, *assafeer*, to the Egyptians, are much loved as a *meze*, seasoned and grilled over charcoal braziers, served sprinkled with lemon juice. Once I had overcome my initial qualms as to their teeniness – I too enjoyed them. English quail are guttsier in flavour, which I like. But you could substitute baby poussins – one will do 2–4 people.

SERVES 6–12
12 quail, cleaned
1–2 garlic cloves, skinned and very finely chopped
Maldon or sea salt
10 ml (2 tsp) cumin seeds
10 ml (2 tsp) coriander seeds
30 ml (2 tbsp) fresh coriander leaves
juice of 1 onion
pinch of cayenne pepper or two of paprika
120 ml (8 tbsp) olive oil
finely chopped parsley
To serve
parsley
lemon wedges

Wash the quail and put in a deep dish. Lightly bash the chopped garlic with a little salt – you don't want it completely crushed but you do want to release some of the juice. Grind the cumin and coriander seeds in a spice grinder and mix into the garlic, then quickly grind the coriander leaves and add them too.

Mix in the onion juice, cayenne or paprika, then stir in the oil to make quite a thick paste. Smear all over the birds and leave them to marinate for 1 hour.

Thread on 2 large skewers (otherwise you'll be forever turning birds) and grill under a high heat for about 5–7 minutes, turning constantly, until they are done and slightly charred on the outside. Serve on a bed of parsley with lemon wedges. Good hot or cold.

Habash Mahshi

Stuffed Turkey

Turkeys, of course, come from North and Central America – not Turkey at all. First brought back to Europe by the *conquistadores* from Mexico and the West Indies, they were quickly adopted into the European kitchen. The French called them *coq d'Inde* (bird of India) later shortened to *dinde* or *dindon* (the male bird). The Turks were equally logical in their name, *hindi*, also meaning from India. The sixteenth-century English were, however, somewhat confused both in their geography, and their fowls. Firstly, East and West Indies were thought for a while to be the same place; secondly guinea fowl, known since the previous century, came through Turkish domains from New Guinea to Europe. The new bird was merely in their eyes a larger version of the old, Turkey was near India, and thus was a great confusion born. Notwithstanding its origins, turkeys are popular and abound in the Middle East. Small and scratching around for their living, they tend to be tougher and gamier in taste than the English birds – plump and cosseted. With spicy stuffings, and slow simmering or pot-roasting, however, they make a delicious dish, often served as the centrepiece of a buffet, cut into small pieces and piled dramatically over their stuffing. The Turks usually roast their birds, the Lebanese simmer them in stock, and often add cayenne and paprika to the stuffing.

SERVES 10–12
3.6 kg (8 lb) turkey, dressed weight, liver reserved
juice of 2 lemons
120 ml (8 tbsp) olive oil
450 g (1 lb) lamb, minced
50 g (2 oz) blanched almonds
50 g (2 oz) pistachios shelled
50 g (2 oz) walnuts
50 g (2 oz) sultanas
225 g (8 oz) long grain rice
small bunch fresh parsley, finely chopped
5 ml (1 tsp) ground allspice
5 ml (1 tsp) ground cinnamon
Maldon or sea salt
freshly ground black pepper
175–225 ml (6–8 fl oz) turkey or chicken stock
To garnish
50 g (2 oz) pine nuts

Wash the turkey inside and out, and squeeze over the juice of 1 lemon. Cut out any yellowish bits from the liver, finely chop and reserve. Heat 15 ml (3 tbsp) of olive oil in a large pan, add the mince and stir fry for 3–4 minutes until coloured all over. Add the nuts and fry for another 3 minutes, add the sultanas and then stir in the rice and cook until all the grains are gleaming. Take off the heat and mix in the parsley, spices and salt and pepper, then the liver and the remaining lemon juice. Stuff the turkey with the mixture – not packing too tightly for the rice will swell up, then brush all over with the remaining oil. Put the turkey in a large roasting tin, pour the stock in the bottom and cover loosely with foil. Cook in the oven at 190°C (375°F) mark 5 for 25–30 minutes to every 450 g (1 lb), plus an extra 25 minutes or so until the bird is quite tender. If you want the skin golden, remove the foil for the last 40 minutes but many people prefer the flesh to remain pale. Remove from the oven when done and leave, covered, to cool. Carve the flesh into bite-sized pieces, discarding the skin if you haven't browned the top, then pile the stuffing onto a serving platter and arrange the turkey meat on top. Just before serving, fry the pine nuts in a little oil and scatter on top.

KHUDAR

Vegetables

Lances we have, the tips whereof are curled,
  Their bodies like a hawser turned and twirled,
Yet fair to view, with ne'er a knot to boot,
  Their heads bolt upright from the shoulder shoot,
And, by the grace of Him Who made us all,
  Firm-fixed in soil they stand, like pillars tall.[1]

Thus was the noble asparagus poetically described at the famous banquet held by the Baghdad Caliph Mustakfi.[2] The gathering had been called to discuss the great dishes of the Arab kitchen, each one present to read a poem, thereafter all to feast on the fare so lyrically portrayed. Even then asparagus was a rare delicacy, and it was the one poem not translated into reality, the Caliph calling for someone to write to his neighbouring ruler to 'request him to send us such asparagus from Damascus'.[3] Ten centuries later its appearance in the market place of Baghdad was still cause for excitement, and I well remember the morning when I woke to the cook's shouts of *'yallah, yallah, yallah'* (hurry up, hurry up, hurry up) echoing through the house. He had just received word that the long awaited 'caravan' from Damascus had been spotted on the outskirts of the city – and there was a large consignment of asparagus. I begged to be allowed to go to the market and soon was safely ensconced high up on the shoulders of my favourite member of the household, Mahmoud-Ali. Majestically tall, he moved swiftly through the packed crowds surging and jostling to reach the magic vegetable. Gracefully he tossed a coin high up in the air, and almost simultaneously caught three precious bundles bound in plaited straw, just like the poem 'With links of gold so twine they, waist to waist'.[4] Clasping our burdens tightly, the urgency was over and now we could wander gently through the market. From my point of view, it was a dazzling sight. I had only recently read the story of Aladdin's Palace: now here it was before me – jewels strewn in every direction. Mountains of huge ruby radishes, encircled by their emerald leaves, were flanked by long, darkly glossy aubergines – in their turn offset by tiny pearly rounds of turnip. Peppers were arranged as on the salad plate, in a fan of alternate yellow, red and green; beside were large fair-skinned onions, then their small, deeply purple Italian cousins. Above hung a fringe of plaited ropes of garlic – their fat cloves shining faintly pink through the papery covering. Huge bundles of coriander leaves flopped behind a pool of lemons while brightly shining oranges were quietened down by the soft green of long pointed okra. And all the time, the shoppers – men as well as women – were prodding and sniffing, was it the right shape for stuffing? Were the pomegranates juicy? And where was the water carrier? The sun was midway on the horizon and we were hot. At last, we came across the watermelon stall. A slice of that – deeply pink, cool and crisp – would do to quench our thirst. Happily, we trotted home, Ali to deliver the treasured asparagus; I to breakfast, then to school. It was going to be a wonderful day.

Kurrat Hamidh
Sweet and Sour Leeks

The essence of sweet-sour dishes is not confined to the Chinese. Yet, strangely, this technique in cooking often seems to go hand in hand with a dualist religion or philosophy. In China, they have the elements yin and yang, male and female. In ancient Persia, it was the very old belief of Zoroastrainism. Here, the opposites of good and evil have to be in a state of balance in order for the world to exist. In their cuisine too, perfect harmony is always strived for. So you have the balance of sour and sweet, the mild with the strongly spicy, the crisp and crunchy with the softly fluffy – as in their rice.

Curiously, of all the other Middle Eastern countries, only Morocco seems to have kept a repertoire of sweet-sour dishes. Elsewhere, the taste seems to have been lost.

Leeks we had in profusion in Damascus (Syrian leeks are mentioned several times in the medieval manual, so that hasn't changed) and, after a family friend had visited from Tehran, this dish appeared regularly on the menu.

———— ♦ ————

SERVES 6

900 g (2 lb) leeks
60 ml (4 tbsp) olive oil
2 garlic cloves, skinned and crushed
15 ml (1 tbsp) soft pale brown sugar
juice of 1 sour pomegranate, or 1–1½ lemons

———— ♦ ————

Wash and trim the leeks – I like to keep as much green as possible, although traditionally only the whites are used. The leeks we had in Syria seemed always to be very pale and elegantly thin. Cut them in half lengthways.

Heat the oil in a pan large enough to fit the leeks in one layer – I use a large shallow baking tin; add the garlic and sugar and stir constantly until slightly syrupy. Add the leeks and cook until lightly golden, then pour in the pomegranate or lemon juice and cover the pan (use a large tray if cooking it in a baking tin, cover with foil). Turn the heat to the lowest possible setting and stew slowly until the leeks are tender but not mushy – about 10–20 minutes. Lovely hot, better cold.

Bamia bi Tomaten
Okra with Tomatoes and Onions

Strangely I did not meet okra – or ladies' fingers as they are evocatively called – until I met the Sudanese. Then I was hooked. But the Arabs love, grow and cook them too – perhaps they were considered just a bit too sophisticated for a child's taste. Shame, for they are delicious. A word of advice though, when preparing, do not cut the tip end right off – this will release the glutinous juices, loved by *afficianados* but overpowering to the beginner. And, *afficianado* that I am, I still prefer to enjoy the full impact of their flavour when I bite into them. (You can buy canned okra but, whatever anyone says, they are not the same.)

———— ♦ ————

SERVES 6–8

900 g (2 lb) fresh okra
90 ml (6 tbsp) olive oil
225 g (8 oz) pickling onions, peeled and halved
4 garlic cloves, skinned and finely chopped
30 ml (2 tbsp) coriander seeds, crushed
3 large beef steak tomatoes, or 450 g (1 lb) small
*   tomatoes, blanched, skinned and sliced or halved*
Maldon or sea salt
freshly ground black or white pepper
juice of 1–2 lemons

———— ♦ ————

Wash the okra, cutting off any excess stalk but leaving the tips intact. Heat the oil in a large pan, add the onions and cook for 10 minutes, stirring frequently, to colour them. Add the okra, stirring gently, and fry for another 5 minutes, then add the garlic and coriander – push the okra and onions to the sides of the pan, and cook until the aroma starts to rise, about 3–4 minutes, before putting in the tomatoes. Season with salt and pepper (a mixture of black and white for my taste) then add a wineglass or two of water – just to cover the okra, and cook, very slowly until the okra are really tender – 45 minutes to 1 hour. Add the juice of 1 lemon, and simmer for another 10 minutes, then turn onto a serving plate, leave to cool, covered. Sprinkle on more lemon juice if you want and serve.

Jazar Atariyah
Spiced Carrots

My English friends are amazed when I mention carrots as a Middle Eastern vegetable. There is something indescribably British about carrots, solid, respectable, slightly sweet, always there – usually overcooked. Yet in Persia, and Tunisia – the Moorish arm was long and broadly swept – they are a favourite, sweetly seasoned in the one country, hotly, in the other. Their native habitat of course is Afghanistan – not surprising when one remembers how beautifully India treats them: as a heavenly sweet – regally decorated with silver leaf.

SERVES 6

900 g (2 lb) carrots
30 ml (2 tbsp) olive oil
3 garlic cloves, skinned and finely chopped
15 ml (1 tbsp) cumin seeds, crushed (optional)
15 ml (1 tbsp) caraway seeds (optional)
1–2 dried red chillies (optional)
Maldon or sea salt
pinch of granulated sugar (optional)
15 ml (1 tbsp) rose-water
To serve
lemon juice (optional)

Top and tail the carrots, scrub them and cut into long thin fingers. Heat the oil in a large pan, add the garlic and sauté for 1 minute, then add the cumin (or caraway and chilli) and carrots. Toss for a couple of minutes to glaze slightly, then add a wineglass of water, salt, sugar if the carrots are old, and the rose-water. Cook over a medium heat, covered, until the carrots are just done – still with a bite – and the liquid absorbed. Put into a serving dish, let cool slightly, and serve. Some like lemon juice – I think it kills the rose-water, so suit your taste.

Batata Mahshi
Stuffed Potato Balls

Potatoes are not a particularly Middle Eastern vegetable. But they do exist and are occasionally transformed into something quite magical – as here. There is an even more spectacular dish in which a hollow is cored out of the whole potato and the stuffing put therein. These I was given, once – I must have been unusually angelic that day. But they are tricky to get quite right, and I find these 'surprise' potato balls go down so well that I confess I have not faced the

difficulty again. For brave souls – bake the stuffed spuds in the oven – medium setting, half covered with a tomato sauce, for about 1 hour. Until they are soft but not disintegrating – that's the clever bit. I had these in Iraq incidentally, although Syria has her version, but not Persia, where potatoes were until recently called 'Malcolm's plums' after the man who introduced them, and where they are still regarded with some trepidation. In the Lebanon, they use a mixture of soft cheese, meat and fresh herbs for the stuffing.

SERVES 6

900 g (2 lb) potatoes
Maldon salt or sea salt
1 large egg, beaten
30 ml (2 tbsp) plain flour
30 ml (2 tbsp) olive oil, plus extra for frying
1 large onion, skinned and minced or grated
125 g (4 oz) pine nuts
50 g (2 oz) sultanas or raisins
small bunch parsley, very finely chopped
1.5 ml (¼ tsp) ground ginger
1.5 ml (¼ tsp) ground allspice
homemade dried finely ground breadcrumbs
To serve
chopped parsley (optional)

Peel the potatoes, cut them into even-sized pieces and boil in salted water until well done. Mash thoroughly – nothing is more unattractive than lumpy mashed potato – and then return to the pan over a medium heat to dry out for 1 minute. Stir in the egg, then sift on the flour and beat in well to mix. Season with a little more salt.

Heat the oil, add the onion and sauté for 15 minutes until very soft and golden. Push to the side of the pan, add the pine nuts and cook for 1–2 minutes until pink, then pour on the sultanas and parsley. Season with ginger and allspice, and cook for another minute, then pour in 60 ml (4 tbsp) of hot water. Lower the heat and simmer for 4–5 minutes until the liquid is completely absorbed.

Take lumps of the potato about the size of a small plum, roll into small balls. Then poke a finger through to the centre of the potato, swivelling your finger slightly to make a good hollow. Fill with a little of the stuffing, then close the potato over the hole, smoothing over so that it doesn't burst.

Cover the balls with breadcrumbs, rolling them well in, then heat a good 2.5 cm (1 inch) of olive oil in a deep pan until just smoking. Put 2 or 3 balls into the pan, and cook quickly, constantly turning them, until deeply browned and cripsy all over. Drain and cook the rest as quickly as possible. Keep warm in a hot oven while cooking the remainder. Serve, with extra chopped parsley if wished. A pepper mill on the table is a must.

Karafan wa Limun

Celeriac Stewed in Lemon

Celeriac, the celery brainwashed by botanists to grow like a turnip. It has survived this brutal treatment remarkably well to give us the sweetness of one, and the smoky pepperiness of the other – a lovely vegetable, and a perfect partner to lemon. A good Lebanese marriage.

SERVES 4–6
2–3 large celeriacs
60–75 ml (4–5 tbsp) olive oil
pinch of cinnamon
pinch of paprika
tiny pinch of cayenne
juice of 1½–2 lemons
Maldon or sea salt
freshly ground black pepper

Peel the celeriacs – they are often quite pitted so you may need to peel deeply, don't feel too guilty. Cut into slices, then into long thin matchsticks. Heat the oil in a large shallow pan, add the celeriac and fry, turning constantly, until lightly golden all over. Pour in about a wineglass of water, sprinkle on the spices, then the juice of 1½ lemons. Simmer for about 20 minutes, then taste the liquid – if it needs more lemon, add it. Season with salt and black pepper if you wish – not too much though, the cayenne is quite spicy and you don't want to kill the delicate balance of tastes. Cook for another 10 minutes or until the celeriac is tender. I think best cold, although often served hot.

Baklalı Enginar

Artichoke Hearts with Broad Beans

Artichokes are beloved of the Greeks and Turks. Also, interestingly, of the Copts – who observe the most devout Lenten fast. It reminds me of medieval Venice – no meat, no milk, no butter, no eggs, no cheese. Much ingenuity was needed to provide interesting food during those 40 days. And it was given. This dish is almost too good for the *meze* table. It should be appreciated on its own. Certainly the English climate is not forgiving enough to give it to us in Lent. So, enjoy it in early summer, as the Greeks and Turks do.

SERVES 6
6 fresh artichokes
juice of 2 lemons
45 ml (3 tbsp) olive oil
2–3 garlic cloves, skinned and finely chopped
pinch of granulated sugar
700 g (1½ lb) fresh broad beans, shelled
15 ml (1 tbsp) finely chopped marjoram
Maldon or sea salt
freshly ground black pepper

The fresher the artichokes the better. If you can pick your own, you will be able to prepare them easily the traditionalist way – removing the leaves, then scraping out the choke to leave just the heart. If you have to buy your artichokes, I find it easier to throw them into a pan of boiling water and cook for 5–7 minutes. This makes light work of peeling the leaves and pulling out the choke (*do not* throw the leaves away – once peeled, cook them for a further 5 minutes and enjoy them – dipped into a mustardy vinaigrette – cook's perks!). Put the hearts into a large pan with the lemon juice, oil, garlic, sugar and about 175 ml (6 fl oz) of water. Bring to the boil, then add the shelled broad beans, marjoram, salt and black pepper. Turn the heat low and simmer for about 30–40 minutes until artichokes and beans are tender, by which time the liquid will be much reduced. Transfer vegetables and liquid to a serving dish – leave to cool to room temperature. Eat every day of Lent – it will pass quickly.

Patlıcanli Hellim
Fried Aubergines with Cheese

Aubergines come in all shapes and sizes in the Middle East – and a rainbow of colours, from the palest ivory to the glossiest purple-black. Heavily speckled, pale purple and dark, dark black aubergines are sometimes regarded as bad luck for young women, said to cause sterility should they touch one. Yet in Syria, and I believe, in Egypt, to walk slowly round, and through, a plot of growing aubergines is said to cure that same sterility. Strange how folklore develops. In Turkey they are enjoyed as the delicious food they are. Particularly good, though rich, in this dish. If you cannot obtain Hellim – known as Halumi in Greek delicatessens – use Mozzarella, similar in taste and texture, but dry it for a day first.

———————◆———————

SERVES 6–8

2 large aubergines, long and thin
Maldon or sea salt
60–120 ml (4–8 tbsp) olive oil, plus extra for
   frying
225 g (8 oz) Hellim cheese
4 eggs, beaten
freshly ground black pepper
60 ml (4 tbsp) finely chopped parsley
15 ml (1 tbsp) dill seeds, crushed
homemade dried white breadcrumbs, finely ground
To serve
lemon wedges

———————◆———————

Cut the stem off the aubergines, then cut in half lengthways chopping each half into three or four pieces. Put on a plate, sprinkle with salt and leave for 30–45 minutes, then rinse thoroughly and pat dry.

Heat the oil (the lesser amount) in a large frying pan, add the aubergines and fry quickly on both sides just to colour them. Add more oil if necessary when turning them. Drain on absorbent kitchen paper.

Grate the Hellim into a bowl, add 2 of the eggs, freshly ground black pepper, the parsley and dill and mix well. Sandwich two slices of aubergine with a little of the cheese mixture – don't worry they will not fall apart, then dip each parcel into the remaining eggs, then coat very well with breadcrumbs. Heat a good 5 cm (2 inches) of oil in a large pan until just smoking, then add 2 parcels and fry for 2–3 minutes until golden and crispy. Drain very well, cook the rest and serve at once. Lemon wedges to accompany.

Imam Bayaldi
Stuffed Aubergines

One of the most famous of the Turkish *mezeler*, its name literally means 'the Imam fainted' – some say with pleasure at the deliciousness of the dish, others claim the poor priest was horrified at the amount of oil the dish used. I prefer the first theory, especially as you can overcome the problem of aubergines soaking up too much oil by salting them first. This also draws out much of the bitter juices which would otherwise spoil the dish. There are many other versions of stuffed aubergine – *badinjan mahshi* to the Arabs, some using minced lamb or beef and pine nuts (particularly popular in Syria and Lebanon), cheese and minced lamb (Turkey), or rice, and minced meat (everywhere), or nuts (all over).

———————◆———————

SERVES 4–8

4 medium-sized aubergines, preferably long and
   slim
Maldon or sea salt
150 ml (¼ pint) olive oil
2 large onions, skinned and finely chopped
3 garlic cloves, skinned and crushed
good bunch parsley, finely chopped
3 large tomatoes, blanched, skinned and coarsely
   chopped
1 bay leaf
2.5 ml (½ tsp) ground cinnamon
freshly ground black pepper
2.5–5 ml (½–1 tsp) caster sugar
juice of 1 large lemon
To garnish
50 g (2 oz) black olives, stoned and halved

———————◆———————

Cut the stems off the aubergines, then slice each aubergine in half lengthways and scoop out some of the flesh – make a deepish hollow but leave a little flesh around the edges of the skins or they can break very easily. Sprinkle the insides with salt, and the pile of scooped-out flesh, and leave for at least 30 minutes.

Heat 45 ml (3 tbsp) of the oil in a frying pan, add the onions and sauté for about 10 minutes until soft and golden. Add the crushed garlic and fry for another 2 minutes, then stir in the parsley, tomatoes, bay leaf and cinnamon. Season with salt and black pepper and cook for another 5 minutes, until the tomatoes are soft. Pile into a bowl and cool slightly.

Wash the aubergines gently to remove the salt, put the flesh into a sieve and rinse in cold water, then squeeze to dry. Drain the aubergine shells, and pat dry as much as possible. Add another 30 ml (2 tbsp) of oil to the frying pan, and quickly cook the flesh for 2–3 minutes. Add to the onion mixture. Pour in another 30 ml (2 tbsp) of oil to the pan and sauté the shells, skin sides, for a couple of minutes, then carefully arrange, side by side in a pan into which they fit snugly. Spoon some stuffing into each one, then mix the remaining oil with about 150 ml (¼ pint) of water and the sugar and lemon juice and pour, carefully, over the aubergines. Add a little more water if necessary – they should be just covered.

Cover the pan, and simmer very gently until the aubergines are quite soft, about 30–45 minutes. Take off the heat and let them cool in the pan, then transfer, with care, to a serving dish and garnish with black olives. Serve at room temperature. Can be kept in the refrigerator up to 6 hours before serving.

Manitaria
Greek Mushrooms in Oil

Mushrooms *à la grecque* must be one of the most famous *meze* dishes in the world. Unfortunately, too often it suffers from over-designing. It is at its best when simple – nice firm mushrooms, good olive oil, lemon, garlic, parsley and thyme. Water is used in the simplest versions, white wine in more sophisticated recipes. Either is good, but you do not need anything else.

◆

SERVES 6–8
1 kg (1¼ lb) tiny button mushrooms
150 ml (¼ pint) olive oil
125 ml (4 fl oz) white wine
Maldon or sea salt
freshly ground black pepper
1 sprig fresh thyme
2 garlic cloves, skinned and very finely chopped
small bunch parsley, finely chopped
juice of 1–1½ large lemons

◆

Wipe the mushrooms with a damp cloth. Mix together all the remaining ingredients, except the juice of the extra half lemon in a large pan and bring to the boil. Turn the heat down, add the mushrooms, stir around, then simmer very gently for 6–10 minutes until the mushrooms are tender. Transfer to a serving dish and let them completely cool – vital for the flavours to mellow. Serve with good bread to mop up the delicious juices.

Fassolakia Freska
Green Beans with Onion and Tomato

Beans, beans, everywhere. All over the Middle East they grow. And there are countless ways of preserving them, and cooking them. We had them in salads, we had them as a vegetable, we had them in *eggahs*. Packed in huge jars and salted – they stared at us balefully through their glass in the winter. I still love green beans and only lament at the eccentricities of the English summer which sometimes gives me a glut or, as this year, only five. Not pounds – beans. Onions, thankfully, I can leave to the ace-grower in my village.

A Greek recipe this, but popular also in Turkey – with cinnamon and coriander; the Lebanon – with cinnamon, paprika and cayenne; Persia – with dill and garlic; Iraq – with garlic and fresh coriander. I like it too with fresh pineapple, mint and garlic.

◆

SERVES 6
1 kg (2¼ lb) fresh green beans
60 ml (4 tbsp) olive oil
2 large onions, skinned and finely sliced
1 garlic clove, skinned and finely chopped
30 ml (2 tbsp) tomato purée
15 ml (1 tbsp) dried rigani or oregano
Maldon or sea salt
freshly ground black pepper
To serve
lemon wedges (optional)

◆

Top and tail the beans, then cut into long diagonal slices. Heat the oil in a large shallow pan, add the onions and fry for 10 minutes until softened. Add the garlic and cook for another minute. Mix the tomato purée with about 2 wineglasses of water and stir into the pan. Add the beans – the water should cover them, if not, add a little more. Sprinkle with rigani, salt and pepper (white in Iraq – which I still favour), cover the pan and simmer, very slowly, for about 20–40 minutes, depending on the age and the origin of your beans. Serve hot or cold, with lemon wedges if wished.

Chourba wa Tomatin

Courgettes baked with tomatoes

Courgettes are a much used vegetable all over the Middle East – and much attention is paid when buying them. For stuffing, they should be large and oval. For salads, long and thin. For this dish, slim and fairly small. It is quite an art – the only thing that would flummox the Arab housewife would be the English prize marrow. And yet this recipe, particularly loved in Turkey, is the perfect answer to those whoppers.

SERVES 6
900 g (2 lb) courgettes
90 ml (6 tbsp) olive oil
2–3 garlic cloves, skinned and finely chopped
450 g (1 lb) fresh small tomatoes, blanched, skinned and halved
15 ml (1 tbsp) coriander seeds, crushed
Maldon or sea salt
freshly ground black pepper
finely chopped parsley (optional)
lemon juice (optional)

Top and tail the courgettes – if they are small, merely cut down the middle, lengthways, otherwise cut into thick slices. Heat the oil, add the garlic and sauté for ½ minute – take care here, garlic burns very easily. Add the courgettes and fry for another 2–3 minutes, turning fairly frequently to colour them. Add the tomatoes, stir for 1 minute, then bash slightly with a wooden spoon to release their juices. Sprinkle over the coriander seeds, salt and black pepper, cover the pan and simmer – very gently – for about 10–15 minutes until the courgettes are done – but not slushy, they should still have just a bite to them. Put into a serving dish, allow to cool, then sprinkle with parsley and lemon juice if wished.

Basal Malfoul

Stuffed Onions

Onions are not just used as a basic flavouring ingredient, or eaten raw, alone and in salads. They are also candidates for stuffing, appearing with different fillings in almost every country. I particularly like the mixture we had in Baghdad – though I think it has Turkish overtones. The sweetness of the sultanas, pine nuts and mint complements the onions perfectly but any of the traditional stuffing mixtures are good. In Saudi Arabia they turn this into a truly regal dish, which is well worth doing once in a while – but be warned, you need time and patience. For the onions are slashed through to the centre onced peeled, then boiled for about 10 minutes until softening and the layers starting to separate. Each 'leaf' is then stuffed, rolled and tied with string, lightly sautéed and then simmered until soft. Perfect for the *meze* table. But for small gatherings, or if time is of the essence, the version below is quicker and simpler. Still delicious.

SERVES 6–12
12 medium onions, skinned
100 g (4 oz) pine nuts
30 ml (2 tbsp) olive oil
75 g (3 oz) long grain rice, well rinsed and drained
50 g (2 oz) sultanas or raisins
2 medium tomatoes, blanched, skinned and chopped
60 ml (4 tbsp) finely chopped parsley
30 ml (2 tbsp) finely chopped fresh mint
1.5 ml (¼ tsp) ground allspice
Maldon or sea salt
freshly ground white pepper
lemon juice

Boil the onions in a large pan of water for about 10 minutes until fairly soft. Drain and leave until cool enough to handle, then cut a small slice of the stem end, and pull out the centres. Give yourself a decent-sized hollow but leave a thick shell so they don't fall apart. Keep the scooped out flesh for flavouring another dish.

Fry the pine nuts in the oil until they turn pink – about 2 minutes, then mix with the rice, sultanas or raisins, tomatoes, herbs and allspice. Season lightly with salt and black pepper, then mix everything together very thoroughly. Three-quarters fill each onion – you need room for the expansion of the rice, then arrange side by side in a large pan. Pour in water to come halfway up the onions, then sprinkle in a little lemon juice. Cover the pan and simmer slowly for about 25–40 minutes until the filling is cooked and onions perfectly tender. Check from time to time to see if more water is needed, adding if necessary. Allow to cool in the pan, then transfer to a serving dish.

Basal Mamqur
Onions marinated in Vinegar

Onions were grown in the gardens of kings and the gardens of the gods in ancient Mesopotamia, and one of the earliest written codes of law, the Hammurabi, states that bread and onions shall be given, monthly, to the very poor. Perhaps that is why they are so denigrated in Arabic folklore – yet the reality contradicts the myth. Everyone enjoys eating onions. They play a vital role in the Arab kitchen, particularly raw. Even the Prophet Mohammed, despite his strictures not to attend prayers with the smell of onions (or garlic) on the breath, enjoyed eating them. Alas, I know of no foolproof way of avoiding the raw onion's lingering aroma, but the Persians, once again, have introduced a subtle refinement to soften the burning rawness of its taste. Suprisingly, the two potent flavours – onion and vinegar – react with each other to produce this sweetly delicious dish.

——————◆——————

SERVES 4–6

2 very large onions, skinned and finely sliced
45 ml (3 tbsp) white wine vinegar
7.5 ml (½ tbsp) dried mint
2.5 ml (½ tsp) cumin seeds, crushed
Maldon or sea salt

——————◆——————

Toss the sliced onions in a large bowl with the vinegar, mint and cumin seeds. Sprinkle with salt and leave for 1–2 hours, turning every now and again. Wonderful as an appetiser, good too as a side dish with şiş kebabs and köftes.

Pancar Yemegi
Beetroots Stewed with their Leaves

One of the things that used to amaze me as a child visiting England on holidays were the bits and pieces *not* used in the kitchen. Orange rind was the first example that horrified me, since I adored the crystallised peel – one of the few 'sweeties' of my childhood. Then, as I got older beetroot and radish tops – these last are particularly good chopped and strewn on salads. Beetroot leaves remind me of spinach, only slightly sweeter, and make this dish superb. I'm afraid you'll have to grow your own – even if they haven't been shorn by the greengrocer, the leaves wilt too quickly to be any good. From plot to pot within two hours is the ideal.

——————◆——————

SERVES 6–8

900 g (2 lb) raw beetroots with their leaves
150 ml (¼ pint) olive oil
1 large onion, skinned and finely chopped
1–2 garlic cloves, skinned and cut in half (optional)
Maldon or sea salt
freshly ground black pepper
lemon juice

——————◆——————

Cut off the leaves about 2.5 cm (1 inch) above the beetroot, rinse quickly then shake dry, and chop coarsely. Peel the beetroots and slice thickly.

Heat the oil in a large pan, add the onion and fry for 3–4 minutes to soften slightly. Add the garlic if using (sometimes I do, sometimes not – especially if I have baby beetroot, then I just let their own sweet flavour dominate), and add just enough water to cover the beets. Season with salt and black pepper (white in Iraq), and cook gently until the beetroot is tender – 25–45 minutes, depending on size and age of beetroot. Pour into a dish, cool to room temperature, then sprinkle on a little lemon juice. Particularly good with a bowl of chilled yogurt.

Torshi Lift
Pickled Turnips

Of all the pickles prepared in the Middle East – and there are many – this is one of the most spectacular looking and, to me, evocative of both Baghdad and Cairo. Huge jars of sliced turnips, brilliantly coloured by the added beetroot, sit in every shop window, on every café counter. And in winter, there were barrows of hot turnips – pink (from their boiling with the beets) and steaming – on every street corner, the vendors' cry of *mayyi, mayyi* tempting you to a plate at all times of day, to ward off the cold and keep you going until the next meal.

————— ◆ —————

Fills about 4×0.5 litre (¾-pint) kilner jars
800 g (1¾ lb) small turnips
250 g (9 oz) raw beetroot, preferably not much larger than the turnips – 4 should give about the right weight
100 g (4 oz) fresh dates, stoned and halved (optional)
4 small garlic cloves, skinned, very finely chopped
handful celery leaves
62.5 ml (4½ tbsp) Maldon or sea salt
350 ml (12 fl oz) white wine vinegar

————— ◆ —————

Peel the turnips and slice in half crossways. Peel the beetroot and slice fairly thinly. Pack the turnips into sterilised jars alternating with a layer of beetroot slices every now and again, and sprinkling on the dates (used in Iraq, not in Egypt), chopped garlic and a few celery leaves between each row. Bring 900 ml (1½ pints) of water to the boil with the salt, then stir in the vinegar. Pour over the vegetables, making sure they are completely covered by the liquid. If there is not quite enough, add a little more vinegar – you could equally well add a little more brine if you prefer, use 22.5 ml (1½ tbsp) of salt for 300 ml (½ pint) of water. Seal the jars and leave in a warmish spot – I don't mean the airing cupboard, a warm kitchen will do, a cold larder will not. Ready to eat in 10–12 days, check after 10, then keep in a cool place for 4–6 weeks. I have never had any last that long, so more-ish are these.

Limoun Hamadh Makbouss
Pickled Lemons

In actual fact in Iraq we made this with limes – utterly wonderful. But since one rarely suffers from a plethora of limes in England, I have used lemons – also commonly used in the Middle East, and very, very good. Morocco also has her version of preserved lemons. Quartered but still attached at one end, they are then sprinkled inside with salt, about 5 ml (1 tsp) per lemon, shut tightly and packed into jars. The whole is covered with lukewarm water, tightly sealed and left for 3–4 weeks. The zest is used for flavouring *tagines* or the lemons may be finely chopped and added to the salads. This is also excellent with limes – so, on second thoughts, why not be a little extravagant? Make some of each.

————— ◆ —————

Makes 4×0.5-litre (¾ -pint) kilner jars
8–12 lemons, slightly more limes
Maldon or sea salt
10 ml (2 tsp) paprika
pinch of cayenne pepper or chilli powder
15 ml (1 tbsp) cumin seeds, ground
peanut oil

————— ◆ —————

Wash the lemons thoroughly – particularly important if using bought lemons, as most nowadays have been sprayed with chemicals. Cut into fine slices and arrange in circles around the sides and bottom of a colander, leaving the first circle of holes uncovered. Sprinkle well with salt and leave for 24–36 hours (limes need the lesser time, lemons won't hurt if left longer). Pack in layers in sterilised jars, sprinkling on a little paprika, a mere touch of cayenne or chilli, and some cumin seeds between each layer. Cover completely with oil – in my original recipe, it calls for olive oil but I find this rather dominates the soft lemony taste. I have, however, mixed olive and peanut oil very successfully. Seal the jars tightly and leave for 3–4 weeks when the lemons will have deeply coloured and become soft and only mildly tangy. One of the best of all pickles.

SALATAT

Salads

Flowing and ebbing like a swelling sea,
Oil decks them out in cream embroidery
Which, as it floods and flecks them fold on fold;
Twists latchets as of silver or of gold.[1]

I suppose the popular myth of the Middle East as one vast barren desert, with the odd palm tree dotted here and there, is the reason so many people think salad has no place in the Arab kitchen. It is a myth which was obviously firmly lodged in the mind of the new young, and excessively smug, teacher who once told me to be a good girl, and eat up my salad, finishing rather haughtily, 'Of course, I know you couldn't have such things where you've just come from, that dreadful climate, and all that sand. My mind's eye flashed back to the country I had so recently left. How could I explain to this alien grown-up the salads of the Middle East.

The wonderful variety and freshness of their ingredients. The feeling, and enjoyment, of bright colours. Their imagination in pairing unlikely allies, in daring to use the unexpected. Who realised that olives would lend themselves so well to a salad – not as a garnish but as the main protagonist? How did the orange and the onion come to be so happily married? Chance discoveries maybe, but there are so many of them. Simple and gutsy, rich yet delicate, lightly refreshing – there seems to be a salad to suit every whim of the most capricious taste bud. The only golden rule is unblemished freshness – vegetables are coldly crisp when raw, firm even when cooked. Herbs are used lavishly, but thoughtfully. From the palest gold, to the dusty brown of the peasant's home-made brew, oil – in the main – is olive, but always the best one can afford. Its richness is sharply offset by lemons, small, juicy and plentiful. So, at every meal is there salad. Sometimes, only one. Often, many; very occasionally, almost too many. But, yes, we did have salads in the Middle East.

Salatit Khodar Meshakel
Mixed Salad

Since time immemorial this has been known as 'little salad' in our house because all the ingredients are chopped into tiny pieces – a technique so simple, yet powerful in its ability to alter the flavours, which amalgamate not only with each other but with the dressing. I have even tried it simply with tomatoes and onions (especially in the winter when tomatoes can be quite tasteless) and it produces quite a different effect to the same salad conventionally made with sliced onions and tomatoes. The ingredients vary from country to country, and from season to season. Tomatoes, cucumbers, large or spring onions are usually the basics with cos lettuce, spinach or chard, beetroot tops added for greenery. Radishes, celery or sweetcorn kernels can also be added, but keep the varieties to a maximum of five or six (a minimum of three). With fresh herbs and the dressing, that it quite enough – you want the flavours to marry – not fight.

SERVES 6–8

3–4 tomatoes
1 large onion or small bunch spring onions
1 small cucumber
1 small cos lettuce
8 radishes or 3 sticks celery
60 ml (4 tbsp) finely chopped parsley
30 ml (2 tbsp) finely chopped fresh coriander leaves
30 ml (2 tbsp) finely chopped fresh mint or
     marjoram
60 ml (4 tbsp) olive oil
Maldon or sea salt
juice of 1 lemon
1–2 garlic cloves, skinned and finely chopped
freshly ground black pepper

Chop the tomatoes into small dice, discarding the seeds and excessive juices. Cut the onion or spring onions (use as much of the green tops as possible), the lettuce and radishes or celery into tiny dice, and mix everything together in a salad bowl. Sprinkle on the herbs, then the oil and salt. Stir and leave for 30 minutes to let the flavours meld but don't leave it for too much longer if you have included lettuce or it can horribly wilt. Squeeze on lemon juice to taste, then scatter with the finely chopped garlic and season liberally with freshly ground black pepper.

Salata Pimento
Pepper Salad

One of the most popular Middle Eastern salads, not least because it allows the Arab cook to indulge his passion for colour. Yellow, green and bright red peppers are commonly used together, then arranged in circles, alternating strips, fans – anything to show off the colours to their best. The Turks have their version of this dish, in which the peppers are gently sautéed, then tossed in yogurt with a few drops of olive oil.

SERVES 6

1 large green pepper
1 large red pepper
1 large yellow pepper
1–2 garlic cloves, skinned and very finely chopped
45–60 ml (3–4 tbsp) olive oil
juice of ½–1 lemon
Maldon or sea salt
freshly ground black pepper
To garnish
finely chopped parsley

Cut the peppers in half – choose them as long and evenly sized as possible, it makes the griling and arranging easier – then discard the seeds, core and pith. Flatten them slightly if necessary, then put under a grill – very hot – and cook until the skin is completely charred and blistering all over. Take off and wrap in a clean tea towel and leave for 5–10 minutes, then remove all the blackened skin, rubbing under cold running water any places which have charred through to the flesh.

Cut the peppers into long thin strips and arrange in a platter in any design you like, or you can mix them up to make a rainbow salad. Scatter over the garlic, then pour on the oil and sprinkle with lemon juice, salt and black pepper. Leave for 30 minutes to 1 hour, at room temperature, for the flavours to mellow sweetly, then add a little more lemon if wished. Serve sprinkled with finely chopped parsley.

Sarmalahana Salata
Cabbage Salad

Turkey combines raw cabbage with Feta cheese and olives to make this salad – ideal for the English winter table. Other countries also use cabbage, either red or white, often salted and weighted for 30 minutes to soften the cabbage, before dressing simply with oil and lemon juice. And in Egypt there is a popular variation on the Turkish salad, using cucumbers instead of cabbage, onions instead of olives, to give a cool-hot contrast to the salty Feta. All are good.

———♦———

SERVES 6
1 small white cabbage
175 g (6 oz) black olives, stoned
175 g (6 oz) Feta cheese
90 ml (6 tbsp) olive oil
juice of 1 lemon
juice of 1 tangerine
freshly ground black pepper

———♦———

Cut out the central stalk of the cabbage, then shred finely. Put into a large bowl, add the olives – halved if very large, then crumble over the Feta. Lightly whisk the oil, lemon and tangerine juices together, pour over and toss. Season with pepper – you are unlikely to need salt as the cheese is salty, and serve within 2 hours or the cabbage starts to go limp.

Salata Chourba wa Kuzbari Taza
Courgette and Fresh Coriander Salad

In Baghdad we had a marvellous irrigation system of little canals with the gates all over the garden. When you wanted to water a particular patch, the gate was simply opened and in poured the water. Basking in the hot sun, with their daily drink, courgettes grew apace and I would rush down in the afternoons, after my compulsory siesta, to see how many had 'grown-up' since the day before. We still picked these 'grown-ups' very small since, by the morrow they would have already been too large for the cook's pleasure. With fresh coriander leaves, they make one of the nicest summer salads I know.

SERVES 6
450 g (1 lb) courgettes, as small as possible
90–120 ml (6–8 tbsp) fresh coriander leaves, finely chopped
45–60 ml (3–4 tbsp) olive oil
juice of ½–1 lemon
squeeze of fresh orange juice
Maldon or sea salt
freshly ground white pepper

———♦———

Top and tail the courgettes, then slice fairly finely. Strew over the coriander leaves then, just before serving, sprinkle on oil, lemon juice and a touch of orange. Season with salt and pepper. Excellent.

Salata Ispanakh
Spinach Salad

To the Arabs there are no distinctions between vegetables and 'salad vegetables' – if it tastes good cold, why not a salad? Spinach is a prime candidate, popular everywhere. We used to have it in Iraq, raw when very young, lightly stewed when older, with onions and lime juice. The Turks marry it with yogurt, the Persians with nuts, the Lebanese with a simple oil and lemon dressing. Perpetual Beet, also called New Zealand Spinach, is the easiest of plants to grow and flourishes throughout the winter, making this a dish for all seasons. If picking your own spinach to use raw, you will only need half the quantity given below.

———♦———

SERVES 6
900 g (2 lb) fresh spinach
1 large onion, skinned and very finely sliced
juice of 3–4 limes
30 ml (2 tbsp) olive oil
Maldon or sea salt
freshly ground white or black pepper

———♦———

Wash the spinach quite thoroughly, discarding any tough stems and tatty leaves. If using raw, shake dry, then merely chop finely and put into a bowl. Otherwise, put the chopped spinach, still moist, into a large pan with 15–30 ml (1–2 tbsp) of water at the bottom and let it stew gently for about 7–10 minutes. It should be tender but not sloppy. Drain well and put in a bowl. Add the onion, then sprinkle with the lime juice and oil. Season with salt and pepper and allow to cool before serving.

Munkaczina
Orange and Onion Salad

Oranges are widely used in salads all over the Middle East – another example of the versatility of the Arab kitchen. One of the simplest – and most exquisite – is the Moroccan recipe which just thinly slices the oranges, then brushes them with a little olive oil. A sprinkling of orange-blossom water and ground cinnamon complete this perfect dish, very good with the highly spiced Moroccan *brochettes*. Additions to this include grated young carrots or long white radishes, both salads being served well chilled. A gutsier version popular along the Eastern Mediterranean coast includes onions and olives with the local favourite fresh herb. I love it with mint but in winter when I often make this salad, and my fresh window-sill mint is precious, I use parsley, marjoram, a few thyme leaves stripped off the stalk, fennel if we're having fish, or – best of all – lemon balm. All are evergreen, even under the heaviest snows a few leaves will still lurk. And any are good. This is also excellent made with Limoun Hamadh Makbouss (page 82), particularly at Christmas – with all its rich foods.

———— ◆ ————

SERVES 4–6
2 large oranges
1 large onion, skinned and finely sliced
100 g (4 oz) black olives, stoned
Maldon or sea salt
pinch of cayenne pepper
30–45 ml (2–3 tbsp) olive oil
finely chopped fresh parsley, mint, chervil, dill,
  lemon balm or whatever is available

———— ◆ ————

Peel the oranges, holding them over the salad bowl to catch any juice. Remove all traces of pith, then slice as thinly as possible and nick out the pips. Arrange in overlapping circles in the bowl. Layer the onions on top and then scatter on the olives – cut them in half if they're huge. Sprinkle with salt and a touch of cayenne, then dribble over the oil. Strew, fairly liberally with the fresh herb of your choice – very finely chopped.

Caçik
Cucumber and Yogurt Salad

One of the most cooling salads of the whole region, very similar to the Indian *raita*. This is from Turkey, the Lebanese omit the cucumber and add huge amounts of fresh mint, in Persia they substitute fresh dill for the mint and add sultanas, while in Iraq we used fresh coriander leaves. Very popular whatever the variation.

———— ◆ ————

SERVES 6
1 large cucumber
Maldon or sea salt
3–4 garlic cloves, skinned
450 ml (¾ pint) natural yogurt
45–60 ml (3–4 tbsp) olive oil
30 ml (2 tbsp) dried mint

———— ◆ ————

Peel the cucumber and cut into small dice, then put in a colander and sprinkle with salt. Leave for 30 minutes – this drains off the excess fluid. Crush the garlic with a little salt until quite pulpy then mix into 30–45 ml (2–3 tbsp) of the yogurt, before beating in the rest. Stir in the oil, then quickly rinse the cucumber and shake well. Mix in, then add half the mint. Taste to see if more salt is needed, adding if necessary. Sprinkle with the remaining mint then serve as soon as possible.

Borani Garch
Mushroom Salad

A lovely and unusual combination from Persia, also excellent with large fresh mushrooms.

———— ◆ ————

SERVES 4–6
500 g (1¼ lb) fresh mushrooms
45 ml (3 tbsp) olive oil
1 sweet onion, skinned and finely chopped
1–2 garlic cloves, skinned and finely chopped
Maldon or sea salt
freshly ground black pepper
juice of 1 lime
300 ml (½ pint) natural yogurt
30 ml (2 tbsp) dried mint or dried dill

———— ◆ ————

Wipe the mushrooms with a damp cloth and trim off any tough stalks, then slice them quite thickly. Heat the oil in a large pan, add the onion and fry gently for about 10 minutes until softened but only very lightly coloured. Add the garlic and sauté for another 2–3 minutes, then toss in the mushrooms and cook for 2–4 minutes, constantly moving them around. They should still have a slight bite to them. Pour into a bowl, season with salt and pepper then stir in the lime juice. Leave to cool. Just before serving, toss the mushrooms in the yogurt and sprinkle with dried mint or dill.

Salatit El Loubdieh

Green Bean Salad

Very simple – and like all things simple, very good. Popular all over the Middle East where French beans are the ones traditionally used. I also use home grown runner beans, picking them when really tiny and pencil slim. If you grow peas, you can substitute those too at the mange-tout stage when they are quite flat – all pod and no pea! Broad beans are often used in Egypt, and this is the one instance where the frozen article can also be successfully used – though baby, garden-picked ones are obviously the best.

————— ◆ —————

SERVES 4–6

450 g (1 lb) young French beans
60 ml (4 tbsp) olive oil
Maldon or sea salt
juice of 1 lemon or 2 limes
1–2 garlic cloves, skinned and very finely chopped
45 ml (3 tbsp) very finely chopped parsley or fresh
    coriander leaves

————— ◆ —————

Top and tail the beans – if they need stringing they are no good for this salad. Coat a wide shallow pan with 15 ml (1 tbsp) of the oil, then put in the beans. Just cover them with water and sprinkle on a little salt. Cook from 5–20 minutes, shaking the pan from time to time to prevent sticking. I like the beans still with a good bite to them and my baby creatures only take a few minutes. Larger, bought ones will obviously take longer so, check to suit your taste. Drain and put in a serving dish. Toss in the rest of the oil and lemon or lime juice while still warm, then leave to cool. Sprinkle with the garlic and parsley – best of all, fresh coriander.

Meslalla

Olive Salad

While olives of all possible shapes and sizes appear on tables everywhere, two countries – interestingly enough, at opposite ends of the geographical spectrum – also turn them into a salad. In Turkey, very fresh green olives are stoned, then mashed with crushed garlic and coriander seed, while in Morocco the North African love of spiciness is married to finely chopped preserved olives. Both these salads I discovered in London, with Turkish and Moroccan friends respectively, and I must admit I did feel they might be a little overwhelming. Slightly illogical as, it was gently pointed out to me, I can happily devour a whole bowl of olives in a not inordinate length of time – so, why not an olive salad? Why not, indeed. It is excellent, particularly with pitta and grilled meats. If you buy olives in brine rinse the brine off thoroughly before chopping the olives. Olives soaked in oil can be prepared straightaway – you will merely need less oil in the dressing.

————— ◆ —————

SERVES 6–8

450 g (1 lb) large green, black or violet olives
1 large garlic clove, skinned
2.5 ml (½ tsp) cumin seeds
5 ml (1 tsp) paprika
pinch of chilli powder or cayenne pepper
peanut oil
juice of 2 lemons
Maldon or sea salt
To garnish
finely chopped lemon verbena or fresh parsley

————— ◆ —————

Stone the olives, then chop them finely. Crush the garlic with the cumin seeds, then mix with the paprika, chilli powder or cayenne. Moisten with about 15 ml (1 tbsp) of oil then stir into the olives, mixing in very thoroughly. Add the juice of 1 lemon, again stirring in well, then a pinch of salt (many olives are already very salty, so take care). Taste, and add more oil, or lemon juice until the balance is right – there should be a distinct tang without it being too sharp. Pile into a serving dish and sprinkle with lemon verbena if you grow it – this is the traditional herb, and it lends a wonderfully sweet lemony flavour, or parsley, also used by many Moroccans.

Tabbuleh
Burghul Salad

This is one of the glories of the Middle East. Lebanese in origin, everyone now firmly claims it as their own. Recipes are varied and very individual but it should be very green so, lots of fresh herbs. Tangy but sweet, rich yet light, earthy but refreshing, it has all the perfect dish needs.

———————◆———————

SERVES 6

175 g (6 oz) burghul
1 small cucumber, finely chopped
6 spring onions, finely chopped, or 1 large onion, skinned and finely chopped
1 bunch parsley, very finely chopped
45 ml (3 tbsp) finely chopped fresh coriander leaves
8 sprigs fresh mint, very finely chopped or 30 ml (2 tbsp) dried mint
60–90 ml (4–6 tbsp) olive oil
juice of 1–2 lemons
Maldon or sea salt
freshly ground black pepper
To serve
blanched vine leaves (optional)
raw cabbage or cos lettuce leaves (optional)

———————◆———————

Put the burghul into a large bowl, cover with water and leave for 30 minutes. Put the cucumber into a colander, sprinkle with salt and also leave for 30 minutes.

Squeeze the burghul hard in your hands to thoroughly drain it of moisture, then mix with the onions using a fork, and lightly smash some of the onion to release its juice – this will be deliciously absorbed by the cracked wheat. Rinse the cucumber and squeeze hard – pop it in a tea towel if you find this easier, then add to the burghul and onion. Add the herbs, 60 ml (4 tbsp) of olive oil and the juice of 1 lemon. Season quite highly with salt and black pepper, then mix well. Taste. It should be quite sharply lemony but delicately balanced, so add more lemon – or oil – if necessary. Serve, either dramatically piled into a tall cone, or on individual plates, traditionally lined with blanched vine leaves, or raw cabbage or cos lettuce leaves. Either way, there should be a bowl with more leaves for people to use as scoops.

Fattoush
Bread Salad

Originally a peasant dish, now much loved by all in Syria and the Lebanon. I had it once in a small café in Beirut – one of those secret sojourns with my grandpapa – and was full of it when we returned home to Damascus, somewhat to the horror of our cook who could not believe that a restaurant, however simple, should be so cheeky as to serve what was, in his eyes, very much a family snack. Family and friends alike get it in my house, and all come back for more. If you can't get *sumac*, substitute lemon juice.

———————◆———————

SERVES 6

2 Pittas (page 98)
15 ml (1 tbsp) sumac seeds or juice of 2 large lemons
1 cos lettuce, shredded, or 1 cucumber, chopped, sprinkled with salt and left for 30 minutes
1–2 large tomatoes, chopped coarsely
1 large onion, skinned and finely chopped
small bunch of parsley or handful of celery leaves, finely chopped
6–8 sprigs fresh mint, finely chopped
few sprigs fresh coriander leaves, finely chopped
2–3 large garlic cloves, skinned and finely chopped
Maldon or sea salt
freshly ground black pepper
120 ml (8 tbsp) olive oil

———————◆———————

Break the pittas into small pieces – if they are a bit stale I find it a good idea to warm them slightly before soaking – it helps them to absorb the *sumac* water or lemon juice. (Some books say that dry toast can be substituted for the pitta – frankly I find the flavour so different as to be almost disappointing, and I would rather make something else; there is, after all, no shortage of choice in the Arab kitchen.)

Crush the *sumac* seeds lightly in a spice grinder then soak them in about 120 ml (8 tbsp) of warm water. Leave for 15–20 minutes, then sieve, pushing the seeds hard to extract all the juice. Pour over the pittas with 15 ml (1 tbsp) of water, or lemon juice if using, and leave for 5 minutes.

If using cucumber instead of the lettuce, rinse off the salt and shake thoroughly dry. Otherwise, simply add all the ingredients to the soaked pittas, tossing thoroughly. Taste to see if any of the seasonings need adjusting – you may want a little more lemon juice or oil.

Pancar Salatasi

Beetroot Salad

All over the Middle East beetroot salads are popular, usually tossed in oil and lemon, sometimes with a few coriander or cumin seeds. In Turkey they serve it in this yogurt dressing – and I love it like this, the beetroot juices gradually staining the yogurt a wonderful deep pink.

◆

SERVES 6–8

60 ml (4 tbsp) olive oil
45–60 ml (3–4 tbsp) lemon juice
1–2 garlic cloves, skinned and crushed
450 ml (¾ pint) natural yogurt
Maldon or sea salt
freshly ground white pepper
450 g (1 lb) cooked beetroot, skinned and cut into
*   large dice*
60 ml (4 tbsp) finely chopped parsley
1–2 pinches of ground cinnamon

◆

Whisk the oil, lemon juice and crushed garlic together, then gradually beat in the yogurt to make a smooth dressing. Season with salt and coarsely ground white pepper, then pour over the beetroot. Toss quite thoroughly until the sauce is nicely blushing. Sprinkle with parsley and a little cinnamon

Melitzanes Salata

Aubergine Salad

There are many variations of this all over the area. In Egypt they fry green peppers with the aubergines and spice with coriander and garlic. In other countries, tomatoes and onions too are cooked with the aubergine, making a dish similar to *ratatouille*. I particularly like this Greek version though – the crunch of raw onion and tomato contrasting very nicely with the cooked aubergine.

◆

SERVES 4–6

2–3 large aubergines, sliced
90–120 ml (6–8 tbsp) olive oil
juice of 1–1½ large lemons
1 medium onion, skinned and finely chopped
2 large tomatoes, finely chopped
Maldon or sea salt
freshly ground black pepper
5 ml (1 tsp) fresh marjoram or 2.5 ml (½ tsp)
*   rigani or oregano*

Put the aubergines in a colander, sprinkle with salt and leave for 30–45 minutes, then rinse under the cold tap and pat dry. Heat 45 ml (3 tbsp) of the oil in a frying pan, add the aubergines and cook until tender, about 10 minutes. Add a little more oil if necessary. Tip into a serving bowl, sprinkle with the juice of 1 lemon. Add the rest of the ingredients, except the remaining oil, then gradually pour that over, tasting to see how much oil it needs. Toss thoroughly and serve quite cool – 15–20 minutes chilling should be ample.

Kuru Fasulya Piyazi

Haricot Bean Salad

Popular everywhere, particularly in Turkey. Other dried beans can be used but haricot beans are, I think, the best – small and sweetly earthy.

◆

SERVES 6–8

225 g (8 oz) dried haricot beans, soaked overnight
120 ml (8 tbsp) olive oil
juice of 1–1½ lemons
Maldon or sea salt
freshly ground black pepper
1 onion, skinned and finely sliced
3–4 hard-boiled eggs, sliced
100 g (4 oz) black olives, stoned
1 large tomato, finely sliced
finely chopped parsley or mint

◆

Rinse the beans and bring to the boil in a large pan of unsalted water, then simmer until tender but not overcooked – this will take from about 40 minutes to over 1 hour depending on the beans, so check them fairly frequently. Drain and put into a bowl. Dress with the oil and lemon juice, then season while they are still warm. Leave to cool. Taste to see if they need more salt or pepper, then arrange the onion slices on top, the eggs on top of them, then scatter over the olives, finally the tomato slices and lots of finely chopped parsley or mint.

RIZ WA FUL

◆

Rice and Pulses

O glorious aruzza![1] What a boon,
   Thou cook as lovely as high heaven's moon!
Purer than snow that hath been furrowed twice
   By handiwork of wind and frosted ice.[2]

Rice may be an everyday dish in the Middle East, accompanying most meals in one form or another, but that does not mean it is to be taken lightly. Indeed, this staple – once an exclusive province of the rich – is accorded a deal of respect, and a certain amount of ritual surrounds its cooking. Nowhere more so than in Persia, where even their 'plain' rice is half-cooked, then steamed to give a lovely crisp crust before being most extravagantly served with butter, egg yolks and the delicately astringent *sumac*. Its preparation will often have been started the previous day – the Persians always soaking their rice for at least six hours. And the cook will have carefully selected from one of six varieties, the quality appropriate to the dish – and the guests. The best rice we can obtain in the West, Basmati, is about half way up the Persian scale, which makes one realise – with a slight sense of awe – just how perfectionist the Persians are in their kitchen.

However, the main role of rice is as a dish important in its own right, either to be accompanied by meat, fish or vegetables or, particularly in Persia, by one of the superbly blended and seasoned sauces called *khoresh*. It also forms the base of *pilavs*, extremely popular all over the Middle East. Nuts, herbs and/or fruits and vegetables may be added, golden tints given by saffron or turmeric and the presentation is often elaborate, ring moulds being especially favoured for festive occasions – the top of the rice liberally encrusted with nuts of all sorts.

In the curious way that history has of reversing roles, pulses – once very definitely a food of the poor – are now enjoyed as much by the rich. None more so than *Foul Medames* (page 94), proclaimed by the Egyptians as their national dish. Those wonderfully nutty, little brown beans, no doubt gratefully enjoyed as their one meal of the day by the ancient pyramid builders (apparently also given onions to improve their strength) are now eagerly devoured at the highest tables in the land. So too, presumably, was the ancient marriage between rice and lentils, nicknamed 'Esau's Mess' since it appears in al-Baghdadi. The Caliphs had good taste. And even the nomad Bedouin did not neglect his rice – a fertile imagination plucking the one ingredient available from the infertile desert: the date. That indeed is a memorable partnership.

Riz

Rice

Although the minutiae of cooking rice may well vary from family to family, there are basically three ways of preparing plain rice (apart of course from the special Persian *chelo*). These differ in the fat used, and at what stage it is added. For everyday rice, I use the Iraqi version, given below, also common in Syria. In the Lebanon, they add the butter to the water, so the rice cooks simultaneously in the two, while in Egypt, oil is preferred and the rice is fried for a minute or two first, just until gleaming, before the water is added. This method I find particularly good when you want to serve the rice cold as, say in a salad, although I do sometimes cook it the Iraqi way, then add oil at the end instead of melted butter. Choose whichever method suits you best, but always measure the volume of the rice before you start – that means even before you wash it.

SERVES 6–8

450 g (1 lb) long grain rice
Maldon or sea salt
75 g (3 oz) unsalted butter

Measure out the rice in a jug or teacup, then put the same quantity of water in another jug, and reserve. Put the rice in a large bowl, pour over boiling water, then stir for about 1 minute. Pour into a colander and then thoroughly rinse the rice under cold water until it runs quite clear.

Bring the reserved water to the boil in a large pan, with a pinch of salt, dribble in the rice and bring back to the boil. Let it roll vigorously for 2 minutes, then turn the heat as low as possible, cover the pan tightly and simmer for about 20 minutes, until the rice is tender and all the water absorbed. The grains should be separate and fluffy and there will be pit holes all over the top of the rice. Turn off the heat and leave for 10 minutes, still covered. (This applies to whichever method you choose to cook the rice. In the other versions, the rice will now be ready to serve.)

Meanwhile, gently melt the butter in a small saucepan, then drizzle it all over the surface of the rice. Leave for 1–2 minutes to allow the butter to be absorbed, then pile onto a warm serving dish.

Riz bil Lauz

Rice with Nuts

Strangely, I don't ever remember eating broad beans in Iraq, though I'm told we did have them. Perhaps this incredible golden rice, tinted with saffron and crowded with nuts, superceded all other memories. At any rate, I can remember shelling the nuts – a job that seemed to take ages, no doubt because so many of them went into my tummy rather than their bowl!

SERVES 6–8

450 g (1 lb) long grain rice, volume measured
2–3 strands saffron
about 450 ml (¾ pint) chicken stock, or a little
  more
Maldon or sea salt
freshly ground white pepper
30–45 ml (2–3 tbsp) olive oil
50 g (2 oz) sweet blanched almonds
50 g (2 oz) shelled fresh hazelnuts
50 g (2 oz) pine nuts
50–75 g (2–3 tbsp) unsalted butter
15 ml (1 tbsp) cumin seeds, crushed

Wash the rice by pouring boiling water over, stir for 1 minute, then rinse under a cold running tap, until the water is clear. Crumble the saffron, pour over 15 ml (1 tbsp) or so of boiling water, stir and leave for 5 minutes.

Put the rice in a saucepan, with the saffron and its liquid, and a good pinch of salt. Pour in the stock (same volume as the rice), bring to the boil, and keep at a hard boil for 2 minutes, then turn to very low and simmer, tightly covered, for 20 minutes. Turn off the heat, sprinkle with freshly ground white pepper and leave for 10 minutes. While the rice is standing, heat the oil in a frying pan, chop the almonds and hazelnuts coarsely in a grinder, add to the pan with the pine nuts and sauté lightly until golden.

Melt the butter in a small pan, dribble over the rice, then stir in the nuts and leave for another 2 minutes. Pile in a dome shape on a serving platter, smoothing the top, then sprinkle on the cumin seeds. Particularly good with grilled chicken, and also fish.

Riz bil Ful
Rice with Broad Beans

Staying for the first time with my grand-father in Cairo, the smell of garlic frying drew me to the kitchen. It was in fact garlic and coriander, the much loved Egyptian combination, that was on the stove. Added to fresh broad beans, and then stirred into rice, the cook was preparing his family's lunch. Thereafter, I celebrated trips to Cairo with a bowl of this delicious mix.

———————◆———————

SERVES 6–8
450 g (1 lb) long grain rice, volume measured
90 ml (6 tbsp) corn oil
Maldon or sea salt
2 medium onions, skinned and finely chopped
700 g (1½ lb) fresh broad beans, or 450 g (1 lb) frozen broad beans
freshly ground black pepper
5–10 ml (1–2 tsp) coriander seeds
2–3 garlic cloves, skinned and crushed
1.5 ml (¼ tsp) ground cinnamon

———————◆———————

If you have packaged rice, it will not need wash-ing. Otherwise rinse under cold water, drain and dry out as much as possible. Heat 30 ml (2 tbsp) of the oil in a large saucepan, add the rice and stir fry gently for 2 minutes until all the grains are translucent and gleaming. Add water to the same volume as the rice measured, a good pinch of salt and bring to the boil, then boil hard for 2 minutes. Cover tightly, and sim-mer on the lowest possible heat for 20 minutes. Then turn off the heat and leave for another 10 minutes.

Meanwhile, heat half the remaining oil in another pan, add the onions and fry gently for 10 minutes. Shell the beans, then add to the onions and sauté for another 5 minutes, stirring constantly. Pour in just enough water to barely cover the beans, season with a little salt, lots of black pepper, and simmer until the beans are tender – 10–20 minutes, according to size and to whether the beans are fresh or frozen.

When the beans are cooked, fry the last 30 ml (2 tbsp) of oil in a small frying pan. Quickly grind the coriander seeds in a spice grinder – coarsely. Tip into the pan, add the garlic and sauté over a medium heat for 1–2 minutes until the aroma is tantalising. Tip into the beans, stirring thoroughly to blend well in, then add the beans to the rice. Mix, then pile onto a serving platter. Gorgeous as it is, but good too with şiş kebabs, köftes, fried kibbeh and a host of other dishes.

Riz bil Tamar
Rice with Dates

A dish popular everywhere, of Bedouin ancestry, and a good example of the Arab ingenuity with limited ingredients. In Baghdad pistachios were often substituted for the almonds, while for special occasions the cook in Damascus would add pine nuts as well.

———————◆———————

SERVES 6
450 g (1 lb) long grain rice, volume measured
Maldon or sea salt
125 g (4 oz) unsalted butter
100 g (4 oz) blanched, sweet almonds
225 g (8 oz) fresh dates
freshly ground white pepper
To garnish
finely chopped parsley (optional)

———————◆———————

Wash the rice, rinsing in boiling water first, then under cold running water until quite clear. Drain thoroughly. Measure cold water to the volume of the rice, probably just under 600 ml (1 pint), and bring to the boil with a pinch of salt. Add the rice, return to the boil and then continue boiling hard for 2 minutes. Tightly cover the pan, turn down the heat and simmer slowly for 20 minutes.

Meanwhile, heat half the butter in a frying pan, add the almonds and fry gently for about 2 minutes until golden. Take the pan off the heat and remove the almonds with a slotted spoon. Stone the dates (an old book I have tells you to use a needle – I find a chopstick much quicker!) then stuff each date with an almond. Cut in half crossways with a sharp knife, then add the dates to the frying pan with about 150 ml (¼ pint) of water. Bring to simmering point, then gently simmer for about 15 minutes until the dates have absorbed most of the liquid. The rice should now be done, so turn off the heat and leave the pan a further 10 minutes. Melt the remaining butter, pour over the rice, and leave for 2–3 minutes. Stir the dates into the rice, pile on a serving dish and sprinkle with chopped parsley if wished (we did in Baghdad, but obviously in the desert this would be impossible!).

Domatesli Pilav
Tomato Pilav

Delectable hot or cold, with its pretty pale pink colouring. If you can buy fresh plum tomatoes, so much the better – their sweetness and full flavour is unsurpassed by any other variety. Spinach, courgettes or aubergines are often used instead of tomatoes to make an equally delicious dish.

———————♦———————

SERVES 6

45 ml (3 tbsp) olive oil
2 large onions, skinned and finely chopped
2–3 garlic cloves, skinned and crushed
30 ml (2 tbsp) pine nuts
900 g (2 lb) fresh tomatoes, preferably plum or beef steak, blanched, skinned and coarsely chopped
2.5–5 ml (½–1 tsp) granulated sugar (optional)
5 ml (1 tsp) dried mint
Maldon or sea salt
freshly ground black pepper
450 g (1 lb) long grain rice, volume measured

———————♦———————

Heat the oil in a large pan, add the onions and fry gently until soft and nicely golden, about 15 minutes. Then add the garlic and pine nuts, pushing the onions slightly to the sides of the pan, and cook them for a minute or two. Put the tomatoes into the pan, season with 2.5 ml (½ tsp) sugar unless using plum tomatoes, add the mint, salt and pepper. Fry, stirring and slightly beating the tomatoes with a wooden spoon, for 6–7 minutes, then cover with water. Bring to bubbling point, then gently stew the tomatoes for about 40 minutes until very soft and rich. You may need a little extra water, so check from time to time.

Rinse the rice in boiling water, then drain well. Add to the pan, stirring well in, then add about half its volume of water and bring to the boil. Cover and simmer for 20 minutes until the rice is tender, but check after 10 minutes to see if more water is needed – there will have been a certain amount of liquid from the tomatoes, so it is difficult to gauge exactly how much you'll need. Have the extra water simmering on the stove, so that you don't drop the temperature when you drizzle it in. When the rice is tender and delicately pink, it's ready. Traditionally served hot but also, I think, good cold.

Domatesli Fasulye
Beans with Tomatoes

Another good Turkish marriage, popular elsewhere too. I have had it with both red kidney and haricot beans – the latter win on looks, their pale creaminess lightly tinged a rosy pink, but the former on a heightened nuttiness. Try both. The beans may also be cooked without the tomatoes, dressed with oil and lemon and left to cool before serving with raw onion and sliced fresh tomato.

———————♦———————

SERVES 6

350 g (12 oz) red kidney or haricot beans, soaked overnight
45 ml (3 tbsp) olive oil
2 large onions, skinned and finely chopped
2–3 garlic cloves, skinned and crushed
350 g (12 oz) fresh tomatoes, blanched skinned and coarsely chopped
Maldon or sea salt
5 ml (1 tsp) paprika
1 bay leaf
pinch of cayenne pepper
30 ml (2 tbsp) finely chopped parsley
To garnish
15 ml (1 tbsp) finely chopped fresh basil

———————♦———————

Drain the beans, rinse then put into a large pan well covered with cold water. Bring to the boil, then boil vigorously for 10 minutes – *this is absolutely vital* if using red kidney beans in order to expel certain toxins they contain. Reduce the heat and simmer for 1½–3 hours, depending on age and the bean, so check with the package or shop when you buy them.

Heat the oil and fry the onions for about 10 minutes, then add the garlic and cook for another 2–3 minutes. Now put the tomatoes in, breaking them up slightly with a fork or wooden spoon, and cook for about 30 minutes until really pulpy. Add the salt, paprika, bay leaf, cayenne and parsley, then stir in the drained beans with about 120 ml (8 tbsp) of their cooking water and simmer for another 15–20 minutes until nicely soft. Turn onto a serving dish and sprinkle with the basil.

♦

Chelo

Persian Rice

The attention to detail, in all things, poetry, gardens, carpets, metalwork, and paintings – especially the miniatures – has largely contributed to the great finesse in Persian art. So too in her kitchen. Nothing is too simple, too humble, to be left to chance. This attitude is supremely demonstrated in the cooking of rice, from its long soaking to its ultimate steaming with butter and water, resulting in a delicious golden crust at the bottom of the pan. There is further perfectionism yet – in the serving of the rice. The crust, *tah dig* or *hakkakah* in Arabic, is ceremoniously offered to the guest of honour, while each person is given a small bowl of butter, an egg yolk in its half shell and a pinch of *sumac* to stir into the rice. This is considered to be plain rice – to be served with *kebabs* or on its own. At other times it will be accompanied by the slowly simmered fruit and meat sauces, *khoresh*, of which there are hundreds. And for fish, especially fried, there is a further variation, with a handful of fresh herbs – chives, tarragon, coriander, fresh fenugreek, parsley, dill – whatever is available, being added to the rice before it is steamed. This is often served at New Year, the 'greenness' signifying fecundity and happiness for the year to come.

————— ♦ —————

SERVES 6

450 g (1 lb) long grain rice
Maldon or sea salt
75 g (3 oz) unsalted butter

————— ♦ —————

Rinse the rice two or three times in boiling water, then put in a large bowl well covered by cold water. Leave for at least 5 hours – overnight is fine.

A short time before cooking, rinse in fresh cold water and drain. Bring a large pan of water to the boil, add 30 ml (2 tbsp) of salt, then dribble in the rice. Boil it hard until soft but not yet tender. Good Basmati rice will take 8–10 minutes but I have found that some brands of long grain rice only take 4–5, so start checking after 4 minutes. When it cuts easily but still has a 'bite', drain and rinse in tepid water, this will remove any 'oversalting'. Shake the colander to remove any excess moisture.

Melt the butter in a small pan with 30–45 ml (2–3 tbsp) of water, then pour half this mixture in the bottom of the pan. Add the rice, then drizzle on the remaining butter. Cover the pan

with a clean tea towel, then put on the lid, tying the ends of the cloth over the lid so they don't burn, and steam, over a low heat, for about 20 minutes. Carefully pile the rice onto a warmed serving dish, leaving the crust at the bottom. Then scrape that out, and arrange at the side of the platter. Serve on its own, or with *kebabs*, with butter, egg yolks, and *sumac* (page 107), or with *Khoresh Portagal* (page 19).

Foul Medames

Egyptian Brown Beans

'The dish of the Pharaohs' my grandfather's cook used to call this. And indeed it is very old, now acclaimed as the Egyptian national dish, eaten by everyone, at home, in expensive restaurants, bought from street vendors – to be tucked into pittas. Although originally a peasant dish, it has transcended all boundaries, and its appearance on the table will always be greeted with delight. The beans traditionally used are small, round and reddish brown, bigger than a lentil, smaller than a chick pea. They can often be found in Greek delicatessens, and I have used 'English Field Beans' from health shops very successfully. They may even be the same beast but bean nomenclature is rather confusing and I have not ascertained this for sure! In desperation, I have even used dried haricot beans, which proved very good but not quite so richly earthy.

————— ♦ —————

SERVES 6–8

900 g (2 lb) dried brown beans, soaked overnight
3–4 large garlic cloves, skinned and finely chopped
finely chopped fresh parsley or coriander leaves
olive oil
lemon wedges
cumin seeds, crushed (optional)
paprika (optional)
Maldon or sea salt
6–8 Hamine Eggs (page 31)

————— ♦ —————

Drain the beans and rinse in fresh water. Put into a large pan, very well covered with cold water, bring to the boil, then simmer for 1½–2½ hours (this depends on the beans used) until nicely tender but not mushy.

Arrange on the table little bowls with the garlic, parsley, a jug of olive oil, plate of lemon wedges, a small plate each of cumin and paprika if used (in many traditional recipes these are omitted, but this was the way we always had it and I now miss them if they're absent) and the salt. Naturally, there will be a pepper mill – one for white and one for black is nice. Shell the eggs and put one on a plate.

When the beans are cooked dish out into a large bowl and let people help themselves. An egg is usually put into the middle of the beans, then seasonings taken as wished, everything being slightly mashed together to produce that inimitable amalgam of flavours.

Mujaddarah
Rice with Lentils

A very old favourite this, familiarly named 'Esau's Mess' or 'Esau's Potage'. It appears in al-Baghdadi's book though meat was included then, left out now. The name literally means 'one having the smallpox' – as Professor Arberry aptly comments 'a grim jest indeed'. But don't let that put you off – it is delicious, much loved by poor and rich alike, and often served as a course on its own. Since it is so good cold, particularly with yogurt and cooling salads, I often include it on the *meze* table. These are my preferred quantities, but each family has their own, some doubling the lentils to rice, or even vice versa. It's a question of personal taste – and what is in the storecupboard!

I have suggested soaking the lentils overnight, however some lentils nowadays do not need such long soaking, if any. Check the instructions on the packet.

———————◆———————

SERVES 6
450 g (12 oz) large brown lentils, soaked overnight
3 large onions, skinned
45 ml (3 tbsp) olive oil
15 ml (1 tbsp) cumin seeds, crushed
2.5 ml (½ tsp) ground cinnamon
Maldon or sea salt
freshly ground black or white pepper
225 g (8 oz) long grain rice

Drain the lentils and put them in a large pan of water, cover them to a depth of at least 5 cm (2 inches) and bring to the boil. Turn down the heat and simmer for 40 minutes to 1½ hours – again check the instructions, as this will vary enormously with country of origin and age. Top up with more water from time to time if necessary.

Chop one of the onions very finely, slice the others in half circles and reserve. Heat 15 ml (1 tbsp) of the oil in a frying pan, add the chopped onion and sauté gently for 10–15 minutes until soft and lightly golden. When the lentils are almost tender, drain if there is any liquid in the pan, then return to the pan with the onions, season well with salt and black or white pepper (I quite like a bit of both) then stir in the cumin and cinnamon. Measure the volume of the rice, then add it to the pan with the same amount of water and simmer for about 20 minutes until the rice and lentils are tender and the water has been absorbed (you may even need to add a little extra – check after 10 minutes).

While the rice is cooking, heat the remaining oil, add the sliced onions and cook, turning constantly, until they are very dark, almost, but not quite, burnt. Tip the lentil mixture onto a large shallow dish, strew with the onions and serve hot or cold.

Adis Samra Ma' Khudar
Brown Lentils with Vegetables

Another dish with many variations, the vegetables chosen being those particularly liked and/or locally available. In Baghdad we grew celery, courgettes, leeks, tomatoes, so this is how I know it. But equally you could use aubergines, sweet peppers, broad beans, potatoes, green beans or cauliflower – whatever looks best in the market that day.

SERVES 6

225 g (8 oz) large brown or green lentils, soaked overnight
2–3 sticks celery, finely sliced
225 g (8 oz) leeks, trimmed and sliced (use as much of the green as you can)
225 g (8 oz) courgettes, topped, tailed and sliced
3–4 small tomatoes, blanched, skinned and sliced
Maldon or sea salt
freshly ground white pepper
5 ml (1 tsp) coriander seeds
5 ml (1 tsp) cumin seeds
30 ml (2 tbsp) olive oil
1 large onion, skinned and finely sliced
2–3 garlic cloves, skinned and finely chopped
30–45 ml (2–3 tbsp) finely chopped fresh coriander leaves or parsley
juice of 1½–2 lemons

Drain the lentils and bring to the boil in a large pan with a good 600 ml (1 pint) of water for 40 minutes–1½ hours, until the lentils are almost done. Add the vegetables, salt and pepper. Grind the coriander and cumin seeds in a spice grinder and stir in, then cook for a further 10–20 minutes, until the vegetables are just tender and nearly all the liquid is absorbed.

Heat the oil in a frying pan, add the onion and cook fairly quickly until a deep golden, add the garlic and cook for another 1–2 minutes. Stir into the lentils and vegetables mixing well in and let cook for 1–2 minutes, then pile into a serving dish. Scatter over the coriander or parsley, sprinkle with lemon juice and serve. Hot, warm or cold this is delicious.

Humus Ma' Ispanakh
Chick Peas with Spinach

A dish of Persian origin, now cooked all over the Middle East, sometimes with meatballs, sometimes without. There is a similar dish of lentils and spinach, also Persian, and traditionally said to cure the sick. I have given below the Turkish refinement of a yogurt topping with garlic, mint and paprika as it's particularly suitable for the meze table. But you could equally well cook the Egyptian version, in which case fry some coriander seeds with the garlic and salt and stir in just before serving.

SERVES 6

225 g (8 oz) chick peas, soaked overnight
450 g (1 lb) fresh spinach
30 ml (2 tbsp) olive oil
1 large onion, skinned and finely chopped
Maldon or sea salt
150 ml (¼ pint) natural yogurt
2 garlic cloves, skinned and crushed
freshly ground black pepper
5 ml (1 tsp) dried mint
paprika

Drain the chick peas and bring to the boil in a large pan of water, then simmer until soft. This will take from about 30 minutes to well over 1 hour, so check the chick peas frequently.

Wash the spinach, discarding tough stems and blemished leaves, then chop finely. Heat the oil in a large pan, add the onion and cook gently for about 15 minuts until soft. Add the spinach, and stew slowly for about 7–8 minutes. When the chick peas are quite tender, add them with about 75 ml (5 tbsp) of their water to the spinach and onions, season lightly with salt and cook for another 5–10 minutes until the liquid is absorbed.

Beat the yogurt with the crushed garlic, a little salt, black pepper and the dried mint. Arrange the chick pea mixture on a large shallow serving dish, pour over the yogurt, then sprinkle with paprika – a zig-zag design is nice and in keeping with the dish's native habitat. Good hot – also good cold.

KHUBS

•

Breads

'Take first a pair of loaves, of finest wheat,
The like of which on earth was never seen;
Then cut the crusts around, and lift them clean,
When naught remaineth but the supple dough,
Cover one round with fresh-cut slices, so!'[1]

Bread is not an afterthought in the Midddle East. It is, of course, one of the staples of life, as elsewhere in the world. But it is also revered, thought of as a gift from Allah, especially in rural communities. I can remember our cook in Baghdad, muttering a 'grace' over the large flat rounds of dough before they were slapped onto the walls of the oven. This, the most common Arab bread known as pitta to us, is lightly leavened and comes out with a softly chewy crust, an absorbent inner surface, and a wonderful hollow in the middle – perfect for filling with *kibbeh*, *köftes*, pulses and salads of all sorts. These were baked every day at home by our cooks, but in Damascus I would often see children running down the hill with a large flat basket, the dough just ready for cooking, covered by brightly coloured cloths, to the local bakery. Soon they were toiling up again, nibbling on warm *pitta*, the rest safely tucked in their wrappings to keep them hot on the journey home.

That is the most common bread but there are many others, in wonderful shapes and sizes and with an extraordinary posse of seasonings. Sesame seed is a favourite, scattered on tiny bracelets, or small sharp pointed 'sticks'; long flat plaits speckled with poppy seeds are another. Cheese and olives make a festive bread, while a medieval recipe calls for an encrustation of pistachio nuts, poppy seeds, saffron, salt, grated cheese and lots of pepper, sesame seeds, ginger, cumin, the bitter rue and aromatic aniseed[2] – an aristocratic bread indeed. Fancy or plain, bread makes its appearance at every meal, to be used as an eating implement, wrapped round meat or vegetables, dipped into sauces and creamy salads – simply, to be enjoyed.

Pitta

Flat Unleavened Bread

Not just bread, but a container, a scoop, a dipper, *pitta* is the all purpose bread for the *meze* table. Flat, soft and easily hollowed into two, it is wonderful stuffed with *Falafel* (page 10) *kebabs*, salads of all sorts, *Foul Medames* (page 94), hot chick peas, almost anything. Equally good is it dipped into *Humus bi Tahina* (page 15), *Taramasalata* (page 17) or any of the creamy salads. Best of all, of course, with olive oil, and *dukkah*.

───────◆───────

Makes 8–10 pittas
450 g (1 lb) plain flour
2.5 ml (½ tsp) salt
10 ml (2 tsp) Easy Blend yeast
30 ml (2 tbsp) olive oil

───────◆───────

Sift the flour into a large bowl or food processor, sprinkle in the salt and the yeast and mix together. Dribble over the oil, then gradually pour in (with the motor running if using a processor) up to 300 ml (½ pint) of lukewarm water. Take care with the last few spoonfuls of water, the dough should mix together but not be too sticky. Knead thoroughly for about 15 minutes (3–4 minutes in the machine – then the same again by hand) until the dough is very elastic and comes cleanly away from your fingers and the bowl.

Lightly brush a bowl with some oil, roll the ball in it – this helps prevent a crust forming while it's resting, then cover with a cloth and leave for 1–2 hours to rise.

Knock back the risen dough a few times, then break off small pieces, about the size of a lemon. Roll, on a lightly floured board into a circle or oval, about 0.5 cm (¼ inch) thick. Don't roll too heavily or you can make it difficult to split them. Dust each round with a little flour on both sides, then put on a floured surface and cover with a *completely floured* cloth and leave to rise again for about 25 minutes. The flouring of the cloth is extremely important – I once forgot the edges and pittas clung to the towel.

Put the oven on, at its hottest, for at least 15–20 minutes before putting in the bread. Put a lightly oiled baking sheet in the oven for 4–5 minutes. Then put the risen pittas onto the hot baking sheets, sprinkling them with a little cold water. (This keeps them soft but I must admit I – again – once forgot. The result was not a disaster but a gloriously puffed up bread, with a wonderful hollow inside. Perfect for instant eating, but a bit too crisp the next day, although a gentle warming up softened them slightly.) Bake for 5–9 minutes until they smell strongly yeasty. The first time you bake them you will obviously have to check after 5 minutes, but once you know how long your oven takes, cook them without opening the oven door. They should be pale in colour and soft, slightly swollen and hollow inside. Eat warm or cool on a wire rack.

Semit

Sesame bread rings

On our first trip to Cairo, we arrived at night. It was too dark, and I was too sleepy, to see much but the next morning I was up with the sun. Flinging open my bedroom shutters, I looked down on the street below, already crowded with street vendors, busy vying with each other as to the goodness of their wares. Most intriguing was an extremely tall, intensely thin man on the corner, with two long poles over his shoulders, each one threaded with slim golden bracelets. Catching my eye, he moved across the road to stand directly under the window, calling up 'semit, semit'. Five minutes later, there was one happy customer tucking into a breakfast of these crunchy sesame-seed encrusted rings. In Turkey, they are called *simit* or, confusingly, *çörek* which, in the Arab countries, is a sweet bun with raisins.

───────◆───────

Makes 8–12 rings
225 g (8 oz) plain flour
2.5 ml (½ tsp) salt
5 ml (1 tsp) Easy Blend yeast
75 ml (3 fl oz) milk
15 ml (1 tbsp) butter
pinch of sugar
oil, for greasing
1 egg, beaten
45–60 ml (3–4 tbsp) sesame seeds

───────◆───────

Sift the flour into a large bowl, or food processor. Sprinkle on the salt and the yeast and mix in. Bring the milk just to the boil, then stir in the butter. Take the pan off the heat, add the sugar and 50 ml (2 fl oz) of tepid water. Stir, then gradually pour onto the flour, with the machine running if using a processor. Add a little more water if necessary to make a soft dough which leaves the sides of the bowl clean. Knead lightly, then leave to rest for 15 minutes, before kneading again, this time quite

♦

vigorously for 10–15 minutes by hand, 3–4 minutes in a processor, then 2–3 minutes by hand, until the dough is nicely elastic and smooth.

Brush a large bowl with oil, roll the dough to oil all sides, then leave, covered, for 1½–2 hours until risen and doubled in size. Knock back the dough, then break into 8–12 even-sized pieces. I would suggest you make larger rings to start with, as they are less likely to close up when rising again. Lightly roll each piece between floured hands until you have a long thin sausage, then join the ends together to make a bracelet. Mix the egg with a couple of spoonfuls of cold water, and brush the top of each ring, then scatter fairly liberally with sesame seeds.

Oil a baking tray and arrange the rings on it, then leave to rise again – have plenty of room between each bracelet to allow for the spread. Thirty minutes in a warm, draught free place should be sufficient time. Bake in the oven at 220°C (425°F) mark 7 for 10 minutes, then lower the heat to 170°C (325°F) mark 3 for another 10–20 minutes until the bread is golden and sounds quite hollow when tapped on the bottom. Cool on a wire rack.

Elioti

Olive and Cheese Bread

In Cyprus there is a marvellously hearty, rather dark bread full of black olives and cheese. A slice of this soon dispelled hunger pangs after a morning in the sea at Famagusta, which, in those days merely consisted of one hotel and one private house, at either end of that glorious sweep of bay. A tiny, very bent, darkly clad figure appearing from the direction of the hotel, signalled feeding time, and a little old lady would bring a large wicker tray full of these loaves, raw tomatoes and bunches of spring onions for those too lazy to return to the hotel for lunch. It is also a bread popular during Lent, when the very orthodox often leave out the cheese, I have also made it without the olives when needs must and it was excellent. Cypriot flour is a brown-grey in colour, rather like buckwheat flour, but coarser so I mix it with stoneground wholewheat flour which I find gives the nearest likeness.

Makes 1×550 g (1¼ lb) loaf
50 g (2 oz) buckwheat flour
175 g (6 oz) stoneground wholewheat flour
5 ml (1 tsp) Easy Blend yeast
Maldon or sea salt
15 ml (1 tbsp) olive oil
150 g (5 oz) black olives, stoned
75 g (3 oz) Feta or Hallumi cheese, grated

♦

Mix the buckwheat and wholewheat flour with the yeast and a small pinch of salt. (If you omit the cheese you should add 2.5 ml (½ tsp) of salt.) Dribble over the oil, then gradually add 150–175 ml (5–6 fl oz) of tepid water to make a stiff dough. If it seems a little dry, add a drop or two more water – the dough will be quite heavy and should be slightly sticky but not overwet. (This is one bread incidentally which does not make well in a processor.) Put the dough onto a lightly floured board and knead hard until it feels softer, more elastic and smooth – 10–15 minutes. Oil another bowl, roll the dough in the oil, and cover with a cloth. Leave to rise in a warm place for 2–2½ hours.

Knock back the dough, then add the olives, chopped if they are very large, and the grated cheese. Knead quite thoroughly until they are well distributed throughout the dough, then shape into a flattish round and put on an oiled baking tray. Leave, covered for a further 45 minutes to 1 hour until it has considerably expanded, then bake in the oven at 200°C (400°F) mark 6 for about 1 hour until nicely browned. Remove from the baking sheet and cool on a wire rack. Eat within 4 hours if possible to enjoy it at its peak. Otherwise warm it gently for 5–10 minutes. Very good with salad.

Dari Unu Ile Yapilmis Ekmek
Corn Bread

From Turkey, a lovely golden corn bread. And, unlike many recipes for corn bread, it's not too dry since it contains both yogurt and olive oil. Excellent with olives and the salty goat cheeses.

——————◆——————

Makes 1×700 g (1½ lb) loaf
125 g (4 oz) plain flour
10 ml (2 tsp) sugar
10 ml (2 tsp) baking powder
5 ml (1 tsp) salt
150 g (5 oz) corn meal
1 large egg
1 egg yolk
400 ml (14 fl oz) natural yogurt
45 ml (3 tbsp) olive oil

——————◆——————

Sift the flour together with the sugar, baking powder and salt, then stir in the corn meal. Beat the egg into the egg yolk, then mix with the yogurt and olive oil. Pour the liquid, in a slow drizzle to begin with, into the flours, constantly stirring. Increase the speed as the mixture melds, then stir to make sure it's smooth. Don't over mix. Grease a loaf tin and pour in the batter, then bake in the oven at 210°C (425°F) mark 7 for 20–30 minutes until the top is golden and the bread firm. Leave for 5 minutes in the tin to cool, then transfer to a wire rack and cool for another 15–20 minutes. At this stage, I indulge in one lovely warm piece. Keeps well for 2–3 days if wrapped in foil and stored in a cool place.

Zeytin Bittasi
Black Olive Bread

Turkey also has another version of olive bread, no cheese but refreshingly spiced with dried mint. It is much softer in texture, almost cake-like but slightly chewy. Excellent though with thick slices of sweet tomato and a sprinkling of oil and lemon juice.

——————◆——————

Makes 1×550 g (1¼ lb) loaf
2 eggs
150 ml (¼ pint) milk
225 g (8 oz) plain flour, sifted
5 ml (1 tsp) baking powder, sifted
good 5ml (good 1 tsp) Maldon or sea salt
15 ml (1 tbsp) dried mint
45 ml (3 tbsp) olive oil
150 g (5 oz) black olives, stoned and chopped

——————◆——————

Whisk the eggs with the milk and 30 ml (2 tbsp) of tepid water, then gradually pour in the sifted flour and baking powder, beating quite thoroughly to avoid lumps (this can be made in the processor). Add the salt, then the mint and olive oil and whisk again. Fold in the chopped olives – the consistency should be that of a fairly thin cake mixture. Line a cake tin with bakewell paper or grease it very well, then pour in the mixture.

Bake at 200°C (400°F) mark 6 for 45 minutes to 1 hour, until gold on top, firm when pierced with a knife and slightly hollow when tapped. Also excellent – if unorthodox – if sultanas are substituted for the olives. Best eaten within a few hours of making.

MASHROUBAT
•
Drinks

Cool drinks were brought to him and coffee flavoured with amber.[1]

The peoples of the Mediterranean in general and, I would say, the Arabs in particular, are of a very sociable disposition. Never will the unexpected caller, however fleeting his or her visit, be unwelcome. And their arrival will be heralded by the production first, of coffee, thick and strong; often too, by a cooling drink. Sherbets of wonderful hues, sweetly scented with rose- or orange-flower water, creamy yogurt *ayran* or, in Iraq, buttermilk *shenina*, will be served in long tall glasses often encased in a silver fretted holder, and always on an ornately decorated tray. A little something to eat, be it sweet or savoury, then enquiries as to everyone's health, pleasure at seeing the visitor, and a general exchange on life's affairs form a pleasant preamble before the guest may reveal the purpose of his visit. If there is one. Often the call may be merely social – keeping in touch with one's friends and family plays a large and important role in everyday life. The coffee pot empty, the news exchanged, the visitor will take his leave, moving on to his next port of call – perhaps another relative, a business appointment, a message to be delivered. Whatever, a small cup of that steaming dark brew will not be long in appearing. Or it may be tea, particularly in Persia and Iraq, refreshingly made from dried limes (*numi Basra*) or coolingly spiced with mint. Bottles of spring water are a delicacy, especially in Turkey where special trips are often made to the favourite watering place, be it spring or well, and bottles brought home to be labelled, dated and treasured for special occasions. Water, of course, is everywhere a precious commodity, treated with a special reverence, considered a blesssing of God and never wasted, nor refused to a beggar. I remember vividly a huge commotion outside our house one day in Baghdad, a large and vociferous crowd following a bedraggled bearded young man, who was being marched down the road between five policemen, one of them carrying a large galvanised metal bucket. Wide-eyed, I asked what was happening. Nanny's wretched mother gleefully told me he was a burglar and they were going to squash him in the bucket. Tearful, but totally believing, I turned to Ali, asking what he had stolen to deserve such a fate? He of course reassured me that the grisly punishment was a figment of 'Her' lurid imagination, but the youth had stolen the pail, so that his family had some means of carrying some water from the river, too poor were they to replace their own, which had a hole in it. It is an incident I always remember when I see a tap wastefully running. . .

If water is precious, wine is rarer especially in the stricter Islamic states, many of which are totally 'dry.' But of course, centuries ago, much fine wine was made in the Middle East. Turkey still makes some very respectable wines, and so bravely does the Lebanon, even with battle tearing apart her vineyards. *Retsina* is popular in Greece but most potent of all, is *arak, raki* to the Turks, *ouzo* to the Greeks, *zibib* to the Egyptians. Clear in the bottle, cloudy white with water it is aniseed-flavoured and can be deceptively more-ish. You may yet need that small cup of coffee.

Limoun Taza
Fresh Lemonade

Like English schools, we had a short mid-morning break, but unlike our faraway compatriots, we were given tall glasses of ice-cold fresh lemonade – much better than lukewarm milk. It was one of the things that I missed most when I started school in England. At home we also used to make it with fresh limes – a rather wicked extravagance in Britain, but delightful.

◆

Makes about 1.1 litres (2 pints)
12 large lemons
about 180 ml (12 tbsp) caster sugar
4–6 sprigs lemon balm, verbena, or mint

◆

Grate the zest finely of 2–3 lemons, then squeeze all the lemons. Dissolve the sugar in the lemon juice over a gentle heat, start with a little less to begin with, then add more according to your taste. As soon as the sugar has dissolved take off the heat and pour into a jug. Stir in the herbs and chill for at least 1 hour, then dilute with about 600 ml (1 pint) of iced water or to taste. Never fails.

Shai Ma' Na'Na
Minted Tea

This is, to my mind, still one of the best 'coolers' for a blazing day, and a favourite Baghdad drink. The Moroccans have a similar drink made with green tea but usually drunk hot – also good.

◆

Makes 1.1 litres (2 pints)
30 ml (2 tbsp) Earl Grey, or any good Indian tea
75–100 g (3–4 oz) caster sugar
small bunch of fresh mint

◆

Rinse the teapot with a little boiling water (unless it's silver) then add the tea and pour in about 600 ml (1 pint) of boiling water. Stir in the sugar, add the mint (reserving a few sprigs) and top up with another 600 ml (1 pint) of boiling water. Infuse for about 8–9 minutes, then pour into a jug and cool. Chill for 1 hour, then serve in tall glasses with a sprig of fresh mint in each.

Shenina
Buttermilk Drink

Afternoons in Baghdad were joyous. Down to the club for swimming, where the pool was huge. Strictly forbidden for children of course but since I swam on the bottom I could usually get a few minutes in before I was spotted and banned to the children's pool, of which I was extremely contemptuous. However, another little friend and I then discovered the 'canals' which ran around the periphery of the club, about a yard wide and twice as deep. These fed the pools with fresh water and were wonderful for clandestine swimming. Moreover at one point they passed the back door of the kitchens, where we befriended a young Arab girl. It quickly became a regular port of call, for a gossip and a glass of this delicious drink. A similar drink is made in Persia, using yogurt, called *mast*.

◆

Makes about 1.1 litres (2 pints)
600 ml (1 pint) buttermilk
pinch of salt
450–600 ml (¾–1 pint) soda water
freshly ground allspice

◆

Whisk the buttermilk with a good pinch of salt, then chill for 1–2 hours. Add chilled soda water to taste, a few ice cubes and a goodly sprinkling of allspice.

Kahveh
Arab Coffee

The making, and drinking, of coffee is surrounded by ritual everywhere in the Middle East. Introduced to the Arabian peninsula via the Yemen, probably from across the water from ancient Abyssinia where the plant flourishes in the wild, it was widely drunk by the dervishes to induce a trance-like state, no doubt also helping to keep them awake during their marathon prayer recitals – all day, and sometimes all night as well. The (coffee) habit soon spread throughout Arabia although it didn't reach Turkey until some 700 years later, about 1550, when, legend has it, a merchant from Aleppo in Syria introduced it to the court of Suleiman the Magnificent. Despite the hostility of very orthodox Moslems who felt that coffee had detrimental effects, it was greeted with delight and soon became established.

The preparation of the coffee is pure art, and treated with much reverence. The beans are first freshly roasted and very finely pulverised. In the desert, huge brass pestles and mortars are used. The noise of heavy pounding early in the morning is the Bedouin equivalent of our alarm clock, while in Iraq I never failed to awaken to the crunching and whirring of the large, beautifully decorated brass grinder, strategically situated in the courtyard below, right underneath my balcony. The smell of those coffee beans still haunts me to this day.

Once crushed to a powder, the water is boiled in a small, long-handled copper, brass or enamelled pan with a pointed lip for easy pouring. These are called *tanaqa* and come in various sizes, making from one to five cups, never more, and the cups are tiny – similar to a *demi-tasse*. With or without handles, they are often also highly painted or else fit into small fretwork metal containers which will match the tray – again heavy with decoration, often inlaid with a contrasting metal, silver, copper or brass, spelling out a quotation from the Koran. The water bubbling, the coffee is sprinkled over, a cardamom pod or crushed clove added, and it then has to 'froth' three or four times, before it is ready to be served. Important guests first, then the eldest members of the family.

♦

Makes 5 small cups
60 ml (4 tbsp) Turkish or espresso coffee
1 cardamom pod, husk removed and seeds ground
(optional)
2 cloves, ground (optional)

♦

Bring 300 ml (½ pint) of water just to boiling point in a small pan (if you want to make Arab or Turkish coffee regularly, it's worth investing in the special pot – specialist kitchen shops often stock them). Take off the heat, sprinkle on the coffee and spices, if using, lightly stir once, then return to the stove and simmer gently until the coffee begins to froth. Lift up high above the heat, let it subside, then heat again until it foams once more. Stir. Return to the heat for one more frothing, then take off and let it stand for 1 minute to let some of the grounds sink. Pour into small cups, giving each person some of the froth (*weysh*) – a slight shake of the pot should make it pour easily. Do not stir the coffee once it is in the cups. This is a delicately spiced but very strong brew – traditionally the Arabs added no sugar to their coffee, although many now do, making it very sweet indeed.

Türk Kahvasi
Turkish Coffee

Coffee houses are as popular today in Turkey as when they made their first appearance 400 years ago. Many happy hours are spent therein, discussing the world, the family, the local gossip, and playing *tric-trac* – the fast, and lethal, Arab version of backgammon. Always invariably accompanied by steaming hot cups of coffee. The Turks, and Greeks, on the whole like sugar in their brew, and as the sugar is cooked with the coffee, you are always asked which stage of sweetness you prefer, *murrah* (unsweetened, although often even this has a little added – the premise being one does not actually want it bitter), *mazbout* (medium sweet), or *zukkar ziada* (extremely sweet). I use a medium sweet recipe but you can always add more sugar if you wish. A favourite occupation in both these countries begins once the coffee is finished: the reading of the grounds. You will often see the saucer being firmly held over the empty cup, swung round three times high in the air, then quickly inverted onto the table. After a minute or two, the cup is upturned and the fortunes read. Often, with unnerving accuracy.

♦

Makes 5 small cups
a good 25 ml (5 heaped tsp) Turkish or espresso
coffee
25 ml (5 tsp) sugar
orange-flower water (optional)

♦

Bring just over 600 ml (½ pint) of water to the boil, sprinkle over the coffee, then sprinkle the sugar on top. Do not stir. Bring it to foaming point, take it off the heat until the froth subsides, then return again to the boil until frothing once more. Take off the heat, give the pot a sharp knock against the side of the stove, then boil once more. As it foams this time, stir the coffee and sugar quickly, twice, then pour a little froth into each cup and top up with coffee. Sprinkle with a drop of orange-flower water if wished – use a pipette, because I do mean as drop. The perfect pick-me-up when the party is over.

Ayran
Yogurt Drink

Known as *ayran* in the Lebanon and Turkey, simply as *laban* in Iraq and Syria, and *abdag* in Persia, this is a great favourite everywhere – sold on street corners, in cafés small and large, or served to unexpected callers to refresh and cool them after their hot and tiring journey – however short that may have been!

———◆———

Makes 1.1 litres (2 pints)
600 ml (1 pint) natural yogurt
Maldon or sea salt
45–60 ml (3–4 tbsp) fresh mint or 15–45 ml
(1–3 tbsp) dried, chopped and lightly crushed

———◆———

Whisk the yogurt in a large jug, then pour in 600 ml (1 pint) of water, constantly beating. The Turks add considerably more water, their preferred proportions being one to four, but I like it more yogurty – taste and see. Add a pinch of salt, then whisk in the mint – you can make the whole thing in a blender if you wish, for a smooth, frothy effect. Chill for 1 hour, at least, then add some ice cubes to the jug and serve in long tall glasses. Also nice, very un-Arab but I think they would approve the prettiness, is to sprinkle on a few borage flowers. Those specks of intense madonna blue are cooling in themselves.

Abi Anar
Pomegranate Sherbet

A wonderfully exotic, deep purple drink, popular in Persia and also in Iraq. Regrettably, those glowing containers sitting on the café counters, did not appeal to me as a child. Now, without a profusion of pomegranates to hand, I love its bittersweet flavour. It also makes a spectacular jelly. Try to buy plump-looking pomegranates – dry, wizened specimens will have no juice.

———◆———

Makes about 1.1 litres (2 pints)
2–3 large pomegranates
175 g (6 oz) caster sugar, or more
5 ml (1 tsp) rose-flower water

———◆———

Squeeze the pomegranates all over, pressing hard with the fingertips. You should feel the pips being crushed inside, and the fruit will become quite pulpy and soft to the touch. Holding the pomegranate inside a deep bowl, carefully make a slit in the skin with a very sharp knife (do take care, if the juice spurts out, it stains where it touches – badly). Squeeze gently to extract all the juice. Dissolve the sugar in 600 ml (1 pint) of water. Taste to see if you need more sugar – the sourness of this fruit is very variable, adding more if necessary. Pour into a jug and chill well. Add some ice cubes, sprinkle on the rose-flower water and serve with more iced water if wished.

Glossary

The Arab may be vague about quantitites and timing but ingredients are another matter. Substitution is no problem but freshness is essential and great care is taken in choosing particular foods for a particular recipe. There are, however, certain ingredients vital to the Middle Eastern kitchen. The ones that have been moved in this book are listed below. These of course are easily available to the cook in the Middle East, who may even buy his spices freshly ground every day from the tiny stalls – literally cupboard-sized – in the *souk*. For us in the West, this is probably quite impractical but whole spices will keep perfectly well for 2–3 months. Provided they are kept in the dark (spice racks on view may look attractive but the flavours are not improved) and freshly ground just before using, they will retain their impact. A coffee grinder especially reserved for spices is therefore a good idea, and I have also amassed through the years a collection of pepper mills, one for allspice, one for white pepper, another for black, and so on.

Allspice Looks like a large peppercorn. It is much loved for seasoning *pilaus*, and was often combined in Iraq with fresh ginger and a touch of fenugreek.

Burghul Also called bulgar wheat, bourgouri or pougouri and often described as cracked wheat. Cracked by boiling, then dried and crushed; check that health food shop cracked wheat is cooked, otherwise buy whole wheat, wash it (pick out small gravel etc) then boil in a large pan until it begins to open. Dry in a low oven, then grind coarsely for *pilau*, finely for *tabbouleh* and *kibbe*.

Cardamom Very aromatic and expensive relation to ginger. Comes in a large seed pod, white to pale green or brown. Even larger pods, dark brown in colour and often covered with tiny hairs, are sold as black cardamom. Inferior in flavour and scent but much cheaper, and better – at a pinch – than ground cardomom which is often adulterated. Break open the pods and lightly crush the seeds inside. Often added to coffee.

Chervil A herb native to the Middle East, similar to a feathery parsley in appearance,

with a hint of parsley and aniseed in its flavour. Substitute parsley, preferably flat-leaved, if unobtainable.

Cinnamon One of the most important Middle Eastern flavourings, particularly with lamb. Looks like a rolled up piece of bark, which is exactly what it is. Buy it in whole 'quills' and grind pieces in a spice grinder if possible.

Coriander Another highly used spice, both seeds and fresh leaves playing an important role. Seeds, slightly reminiscent of oranges, are dry roasted, then crushed. In Egypt, cooked with garlic, it forms one of the main spice mixes. Leaves are used in salads, cooked and as a garnish: they can be bought from Indian grocery stores.

Cumin Very distinctive flavour and smell, softened by dry roasting before crushing. Often confused with caraway, also sometimes used in the Middle East but this has a much milder taste. Though related it is not really an effective substitute.

Dill Used both for its feathery leaves and seeds, the latter similar in flavour to caraway but more assertive.

Feta A cheese made from goat and/or sheep's milk. The curds are ripened in their own salted whey. Made in Greece and Turkey, extensively used all over the Middle East, both raw and in cooking.

Fila pastry Paper-thin sheets of pastry, made from a flour and water dough, stretched until almost translucent. It can be bought ready made in Greek bakers and is used for small pastries and large pies throughout the area.

Fenugreek Very assertive in taste, can be bitter if over-roasted – do not let the seeds turn red. Grind very finely and use very sparingly for a hint of a curry flavour. Much used in Iraq with fresh ginger and cinnamon.

Hallumi, Hellim Known as Hallumi by the Greeks and Hellim by the Turks this cheese is often used in cooking. It is soft and rubbery when young, hard and salty when matured. Popular in both Greece and Turkey, Feta makes a good substitute.

Kasseri A Greek hard and salty cheese, the curds being cut and stirred then heated and pressed into shape. Good for grating.

Kephalotyrin Prepared in the same way as Kasseri. Often pressed into a skull shape, hence its name which means 'head cheese'. Also good for grating.

Marjoram Sweeter than its cousin, oregano but loses its flavour if overcooked, so add just a few minutes before serving.

Merguvez Hot, spicy sausage found all over Africa, particularly popular in Tunisia and Algeria. Made from goat or mutton, it is highly flavoured with Harissa.

Mint Very important in all the Middle Eastern countries, and often used dried; huge quantities are gathered, then dried in the sun before going into the cooking pot. Fresh it is added to salads, yogurt and tea.

Oils Olive oil is the preferred cooking fat throughout the region, although the ancient cookery books talk of sesame oil, still used by the Copts today: somewhat overpowering on its own for the Western palate, so use it sparingly. For a lighter flavour substitute sunflower or corn oil. For dishes to be served cold, a must, since butter will congeal.

Okra Also known as ladies' fingers in England, *bamia* to the Arabs, *bamies* to the Greeks, these small pointed triangular pods should always be bought very fresh, pale and softly green. Never cut off the tops of the pods as this will release the glutinous juices – except for stews when it is used as a thickening agent for the sauce. A delicious vegetable now more widely available.

Orange-flower water Distilled from the newly opened flowers and sprinkled not only on sweet pastries but often on coffee, and lamb dishes. Available from good delicatessens and chemists.

Oregano The powerfully flavoured wild marjoram, prolific in Greece. Only available dried in England since the climate is not hot enough to bring out its strong aroma.

Parsley Probably the most common herb of the area, although the flat-leaved variety is the norm, stronger than the curly variety.

Pine nuts These are small, slim white kernels of the pine cone, much favoured everywhere, particularly by the Syrians and Lebanese. Sweetly nutty, they keep well in an airtight jar but, unfortunately are never cheap. There is no substitute.

Pistachios Turkey's favourite nut but much loved and grown elsewhere. Pale green, once shelled and skinned, used not only in meat and fish dishes, but also to make a delicate ice cream. Expensive but nothing can really replace them.

Pomegranate Extensively used in Persia from whence it probably originates. Used in cooking, for snacks and eaten raw – scooped out with a spoon.

Pulses The dried edible seeds of legumes, peas, beans and lentils. Widely used throughout the Middle East, for stews and purées; also roasted and eaten like nuts. Traditionally all had to be soaked overnight but many varieties bought nowadays need much less soaking, if at all, though chick peas, small hard and round, and dried haricot beans usually still do. Most will keep well in an airtight container but haricot beans must be used within a year – after that, no amount of cooking will render them anything other than bullet-like. Red kidney beans must always be boiled hard for at least 10 minutes to drive off the toxic poisons. Apart from chick peas, which may be cooked *ad infinitum* without spoiling, check all other varieties after say 30–40 minutes of cooking, unless you are going to purée them. For once soft, they will disintegrate quickly.

Rigani The dried leaves and flowers of another marjoram, stronger even than the wild variety. Can sometimes be found in Greek delicatessens otherwise substitute oregano. Gives the typically Greek flavour to their *kebabs*.

Rose-flower water Very ancient, sweet and heavily scented. Used on salads and meat dishes, as well as sherbets. Buy it from chemists, making sure it's pure.

Saffron The orange stigma from the mauve, autumn-flowering crocus. Can only be collected by hand and is very expensive. Always buy it in strands – the powders will almost certainly be adulterated. A couple of strands go a long way, if you use too much it will give a bitter flavour, and too deep a colour. Light primrose yellow and a sweet honey scent is the effect wanted.

Salt Always use a good sea salt and grind it yourself. If you can get it, use the flakey Maldon salt.

Sesame seeds Small, flat, seeds, which are white when raw. When roasted they produce the nutty flavour and aroma popular in the Middle Eastern kitchen. Crushed they produce the paste known as *tahina*, vital to many Middle Eastern dishes.

Sumac A favourite Lebanese spice where the berries are gathered in the mountains, dried, then crushed and soaked in warm water for about 20 minutes. The resultant liquid is used, the berries discarded. The drink is refreshing and the local remedy for those suffering from 'Beirut belly'.

Tahina A thin paste made from crushed sesame seeds which forms the basis for many cream salads and sauces, besides giving its distinctive flavour to *humus* (page 15), the purée of chick peas popular everywhere. It can be bought in jars from ethnic grocery stores and from health shops. It keeps well. Always stir the thin liquid which rises to the top before using.

Turmeric Sometimes called 'poor man's saffron' since the merest pinch will colour a dish bright yellow. A relative of ginger, and like that spice, a root, although always bought ground. It has a nice, lightly bitter flavour with a hint of hotness.

Vine leaves Used particularly in Turkey and Greece, stuffed with meat, rice, onion and nut fillings. Also much used wrapped around fish to give a distinctively smoky flavour. Can be bought in packets in brine and will keep well unopened.

Yeast Easy Blend yeast has simplified baking. Mix into the dry ingredients and then add the liquid. If it is unobtainable, use 13 g (½ oz) of fresh yeast or 7 g (¼ oz) of dried to 450 g (1 lb) of flour. Unlike Easy Blend yeast, you will need to prove dried and fresh yeast before adding it to the flour.

Yogurt One of the staples of the Middle Eastern kitchen, made almost every day in almost every home. Used for salads, stews, drinks, dressings, chesses. Greek yogurt is usually pasteurised and much thicker – good for cooking but not for making your own from.

Notes

Introduction

[1] Mahmūd ibn al-Husain al-Kushajim; tenth-century poet, astrologer and expert on food. He served at the court of Saif al-Daula (AD 967), and wrote an extraordinary thesis on the etiquette of the table, Adab al-nadim.

Nibbles

[1] A reference to Arabic calligraphy, the points being the distinguishing signs for various letters of the alphabet which would otherwise appear the same; the vowels in Arabic script being represented by small lines and dots, added after the main line of script has been written.

[2] Ibn al-Rumi, a famous Arab poet, murdered approximately AD 896.

Dips and Sauces

[1] Abdallah ibn al-Mu'tazz Dīwān (Collected Poems, Cairo 1891). He had a tragic life, ruling for only 24 hours before being executed in AD 908.

Stuffed Pastries and Leaves

[1] Ishāq ibn Ibrāhīm of Mosul, died AD 851.

[2] Professor A J Arberry – A Baghdad Cookery, Islamic Culture No 13, January and April 1939, from which all the poems are quoted, and also much reference made to his translation of the manual, discovered in Istanbul in the 1930's, written in 1226 by Muhammad ibn al-Masan ibn Muhammad ibn al-Karim al Kalib al-Baghdadi (normally known as Al-Baghdadi). Who he was is a mystery – but he obviously knew his subject intimately and he threw much light on the dishes of the court of Baghdad, many of which were unknown previously.

Eggs

[1] Ibn al-Rumi, murdered in AD 896.

Fish

[1] Abdullah ibn al-Mu'tazz.

Meat

[1] Mahmūd ibn al-Husain al-Kushājim, astrologer and poet at the court of Saif al-Daula (AD 967).

[2] Veal is mentioned, once, as an alternative to 'meat' in al-Baghdadi's book. He wrote it in AD 1226, describing court dishes of Baghdad. This work only came to light in the 1930s.

[3] The effect of the 'fiery furnace' is actually produced by the gases, escaping from the oil wells, below, igniting on contact with the air. There is a slight gap between the earth and the flames – giving the impression that the fires are burning in mid-air. Although we were obviously some miles away, it was a dramatic spectacle – and visible from most of the windows of our house.

Chicken and Poultry

[1] Mahmūd ibn al-Husain al-Kushājim, (circa AD 967).

Vegetables

[1] Mahmūd ibn al-Husain ibn al-Sindi Kushājim, scribe of Damascus.

[2] Caliph from AD 944–946, when he was cruelly ousted and 'had his eyes put out' by the Buyid Ahmad ibn Abi Shuja. He died in AD 949.

[3] Meadows of Gold by Mas'udi, translated into French Les Prairies d'Or, by Barbier de Maynard and Pavet de Courteille.

[4] Mahmūd ibn al-Husain ibn al-Sindi Kushājim, scribe of Damascus.

Salads

[1] Mahmud ibn al-Husain ibn al-Sindi Kushajim.

Rice

[1] A dish of rice (aruz to the ancients) sprinkled with sugar.

[2] Muhammad ibn al-Wazir, hafiz of Damascus. A hafiz is someone who can recite the Koran from memory.

Breads

[1] Ibn al-Rumi, prolific Arab poet, murdered approximately AD 896.

Drinks

[1] Aladdin and the Enchanted Lamp, Tales from the 1001 Nights, translated by N J Dawood, Penguin 1973.

Index

(see also Glossary)